THE METUS PRINCIPLE

Recognizing, Understanding, and Managing Fear

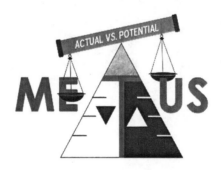

Other books by Brian A. Peters:

The Pocket Guide to Leadership:
The 9 Essential Characteristics for Building
High-Performing Organizations

Not So Common Sense
Threats and 21st Century American Democracy

The Four Noahs
(Forthcoming Summer 2015)

THE METUS PRINCIPLE

Recognizing, Understanding, and Managing Fear

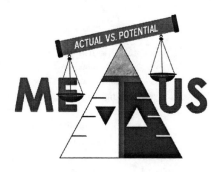

BRIAN A. PETERS

MILWAUKEE, WISCONSIN

Published by
MavenMark Books
An imprint of HenschelHAUS Publishing, Inc.
www.henschelHAUSbooks.com

All HenschelHAUS titles, imprints, and distributed lines are available at special
quantity discounts for educational, institutional, fund-raising, or sales
promotion.

ISBN (paperback): 978-159598-287-2
ISBN (hardcover): 978159598-288-9
E-ISBN: 978159598-305-3
Library of Congress Number: 2014940596

Publisher's Cataloging-In-Publication Data
(Prepared by The Donohue Group, Inc.)
Peters, Brian A.
The METUS principle : recognizing, understanding, and managing fear /
Brian A. Peters.
pages : illustrations ; cm
Issued also as an ebook.
Includes bibliographical references and index.
ISBN: 978-1-59598-287-2 (paperback)
ISBN: 978-1-59598-288-9 (hardcover)
1. Fear--Psychological aspects. 2. Fear--Social aspects. 3. Fear--Economic
aspects. 4. Success. I. Title. II. Title: Recognizing, understanding, and
managing fear

BF575.F2 P48 2015
152.4/6   2014940596

Cover design and METUS diagrams by Melisa Cash.
Graphic illustrations by Jeff Goeke, Transpire Design

Printed in the United States of America.

*May this book inspire you to make changes
in your thought processes and in your life,
to help you become the person you desire to be.*

TABLE OF CONTENTS

ACKNOWLEDGMENTS

I would like to express my deepest thanks to family and friends who have expressed an interest in *The METUS Principle*. I want to thank the countless people who have come into my life and have helped shape me, and my perspective on life, because without each and every one of you, I would not be the person who I am today.

I am a firm believer that inspiration and wisdom can come to individuals, at any time, if they are willing to keep an open mind. The story of the apple falling on Isaac Newton's head and his inspiration about the concept of gravity is a great example of how ideas can come from just about anywhere. Throughout the writing process for METUS, I found myself looking for inspiration just about everywhere. I looked for inspiration and ideas in the books I read, the music I listened to, the television programs I watched, the news reports both foreign and domestic, and of course, in my conversations with friends and family.

I have also come to appreciate that the greater the accomplishment, more often then not, the more interesting the story. People who have reached the pinnacle of their professions, or those held in high esteem, are people who have remarkable stories. When I listen to stories of individuals who have achieved success, I often find myself the most interested and the most engaged in the stories behind the story. I love to hear not only about what someone has accomplished (which is most often reported), but also what he or she has overcome to achieve the success achieved. How did he or she keep going, when many others would quit? How much were they willing to take and put themselves through to achieve their goals.

Throughout my life, I have often considered a particular moment, and thought about the series of events that have led up to it. I think about the people; I think about the element of chance; and I think about the decisions that were made. With each passing year, I gain a deeper appreciation for the concept that, "Everything happens for a reason." I get a feeling that each of our lives has a deep and meaningful purpose, if only we allow ourselves to be open to accepting moments of opportunity that are presented to us and we are able to appreciate those moments and connect the dots.

Through each of the hardships, adversities, and challenges, we can emerge better people, better equipped to handle life's next challenge, when we allow ourselves to do so. We can look for ways to not only better ourselves and our own situations, but to do the same for others. This is life's gift—the ability to connect with other people in endless and meaningful ways.

When I began the formal process of writing this book in 2010, I did so thinking about my daughters, who at the time had not yet been born. I wanted to provide them with insights on what I have learned so that they can use those for what they are worth in hopes that they would eventually help my girls become the best versions of themselves. I compiled my notes from many of the great thinkers I have studied, across disciplines, taking into account the concept of METUS I had created for what was intended to eventually become my doctoral dissertation. I want her to be able to use any insight she finds valuable to help her in her own life—on her own journey.

As I developed *The METUS Principle* into what has become this book, I eventually started to think about all the people whose lives may change as a result of consciously learning to realize, understand, and manage their own fear. Each time I have read through this book, as well as the notes and feedback offered by my esteemed group of readers, I think about all the great accomplishments of those who will decide to manage their fear to accomplish their dreams—because helping our fellow man is one of life's greatest joys.

Even as I write that last line, I cannot help but smile, a most pleasant and content smile, and think about how many people may be positively impacted by understanding The METUS Principle. Writing this book has been a challenge and tested my ability to organize and articulate my thoughts. However, I am deeply optimistic that the benefits of communicating METUS will have a positive impact on people—possibly for you. My hope for my children is the same hope I have for my readers—that this work will serve as a guide for stimulating independent thought and independent action.

I see my work as a lens through which individuals can view their actions, as well as their inactions, with the belief that if they can better understand themselves, they can maximize their potential.

My gratitude and appreciation go out to the wonderful people in my life who agreed to serve as readers and help create this finished product: Dr. Kathy Becker, Linda Braun, Cindy Burleson, Dr. Jennifer Burton, Joseph Ellwanger, Jeff Goeke, Kimberly Krueger, Deb Lyons, Maria, Heather Martin, Jennifer Mendoza, Dr. Ed. O'Connor, Linda Proctor-Moore, Dr. Martha Saunders, Dr. Pamela Schocklley-Zalabak, Kim Sponem, Chris Wodke, and Evan Wynn. Each of you is incredibly accomplished in your own right and I feel honored that you took time out of your busy life and your busy schedule, to provide insight and commentary as they relate to The METUS Principle. I am truly blessed to have you in my life and once again thank you from the bottom of my heart.

And thank you to Kira Henschel, who has invested the last two years in the METUS project.

I have to thank my mom for showing her family what unconditional love truly is. She always stuck by her kids and her family, no matter what. She would always tell us how much she loved us—and that she was proud of us. She enabled her kids to explore, and learn, because she encouraged us to follow our dreams. If we stumbled and fell along the way, she would help pick us up, dust us off, point us in the right direction, and give us a firm push to make sure we started moving again. I could not have asked for a better mom and I hope she knows just how much I love and appreciate everything she has done for her family and how much I learned from the example she set.

Lastly, I would like to especially thank my wife, my daughters, my parents, my siblings, my grandparents, my aunts and uncles, and my family as a whole. You all know who you are, and with each of you, I share great memories that have had a wonderful impact on my life. There are no words that truly do justice how much I appreciate all of you—but if you are like me—I know you feel it.

Thank you,
Brian A. Peters

THE METUS PRINCIPLE

Recognizing, Understanding, and Managing Fear

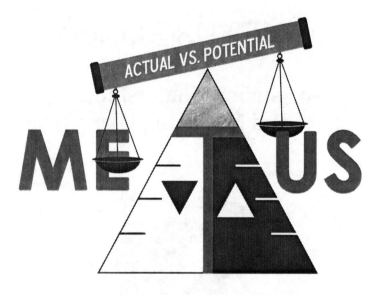

METUS, Latin for fear, is the catalyst for action
and the lowest common denominator for motivation.

PREFACE

He has not learned the lesson of life
who does not every day surmount a fear.
—Ralph Waldo Emerson

The Latin word for fear is *metus* and I would like to begin my book by describing the visual represen- tation depicted on the cover and on the opposite page.

Within the word is a symbolic representation replac- ing the letter "T." Given that many people are visual, and a picture can be worth a thousand words, I decided to create an image that serves as a symbolic representation and visual summary of my theoretical perspective. The image was carefully created with distinct elements, that when carefully pieced together, illustrate the METUS Principle.

The pyramid itself was selected on the basis of Abraham Maslow's hierar- chy concept , designed to illustrate a progression toward an ultimate goal: self-actualization.

MASLOW'S HIERARCHY OF NEEDS

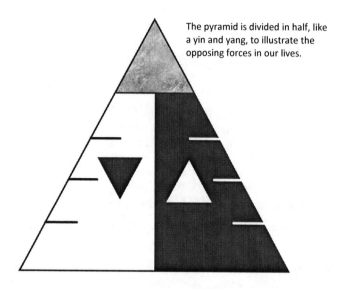

The pyramid is divided in half, like a yin and yang, to illustrate the opposing forces in our lives.

Within the inner parameters of the pyramid, I incorporated the classic Chinese "yin-yang" concept, which is symbolic of complementary, *opposed*, rather than *opposing* forces (commonly misunderstood by many). The complimenting forces, represented by the smaller triangles, are both a person's tendency to fear and his or her ability to be empowered. These smaller triangles point in opposing directions, one facing up, the other down.

The upward-pointing white pyramid symbolizes growth and the ability to manage fear. When we manage our fears and accomplish our goals, we move up Maslow's hierarchy toward self-actualization.

The downward-pointing black triangle symbolizes regression and representative of our being managed by

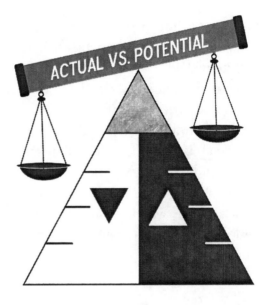

Decision scales weigh short-term and long-term options.

ACTUAL VS. POTENTIAL

our fears. This directional orientation is a reminder that based on environmental factors and a person's perspective, he or she may move closer to or further from, self-actualization at any given time. Just because a person is at a particular level within Maslow's hierarchy does not mean he or she will remain there indefinitely. For individuals to maximize their potential, they must learn to balance their fear. A healthy fear is a good thing, because fear in some instances is necessary for self-preservation and survival.

Atop the pyramid is a scale. The scale represents a person's *actual* fear versus his or her *potential* fear. It is my belief that people will act in accordance with their perception of fear. My concept itself is built upon the assertion that fear is the single-most, fundamental motivating factor in people's lives, and that understanding fear is essential in predicting behavior(s).

If individuals are more afraid of what they perceive as *actual*, than what is *potential*, their action(s) will address their **immediate** fear. If, on the other hand, individuals are more afraid of what they perceive as potential, than what is actual, their action(s) will address their **potential** fear.

The action, or in some instances inaction, a person decides to take, will determine his or her state of being in relationship to that person's ultimate goal of self-actualization.

ME: The belief is in the "I" create my own destiny and life is what I make of it.

Lastly, the METUS image produces two stand-alone words on either side of the center symbol. On the left side, you will see the word *ME*, and on the right side, the word *US*. I want to draw your attention to this because, not only is it convenient, but extremely relevant as we consider various psychological and philosophical perspectives throughout this book and explore the idea of self-determinism versus a collectivist mindset, which plays an important role in the decision-making process, as well as being grounded in fear.

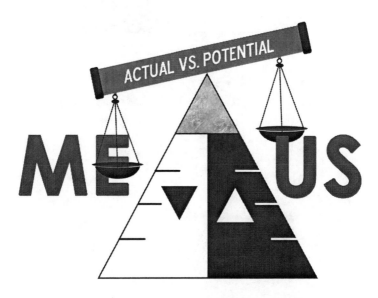

US: The belief that we are products of a system
and an individual is beholden to the system for his or her survival.

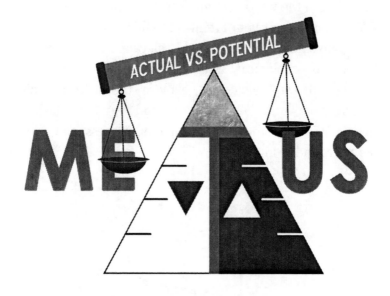

INTRODUCTION

*Failure is instructive. The person who really thinks learns
quite as much from his failures as from his successes.*
—John Dewey

What is the METUS Principle?

It is a way of describing human motivation.
The premise is that fear is the most basic
catalyst for causing behavior.

Where did the METUS Principle come from? It was
created using existing frameworks in the fields of psychology, philosophy, medicine, political science, economics,
education, business, and religion. While each of the
aforementioned disciplines has identified fear as a
motivating factor in some way, none of them have ever
successfully identified fear as the lowest common
denominator with respect to human motivation and
behavior.

Why is the METUS Principle relevant? I believe it is
relevant for two primary reasons:

- If and when individuals are able to **recognize** the
  role fear plays in the decision-making process,
  they can begin a path toward empowerment. They
  can learn to **understand** fear and how it impacts
  choices they make. When these individuals learn
  to both recognize, and understand fear, they can

develop strategies for **managing** their fear in a way that is consistent with their goals.

- If and when people are able to recognize the role fear plays in the decision-making process, they can develop strategies to motivate others to change their behavior(s).

Since we all make choices according to the stimuli in our environment, it is important to know which stimuli have the greatest impact on motivating people to act. I contend that fear—which I consider neither exclusively negative or positive—has been, and continues to be, the single most basic catalyst in determining action and inaction.

Fear is our most innate and basic animal instinct, and as such, is a fundamental key to our survival. Fear guides action or inaction as a person considers consequence. Consequence is not necessarily punishment, but rather simply the result of an action. When most people hear the word fear, it almost always elicits a negative feeling. No one wants to be afraid, much less live in fear. And, for the most part, when we talk of fear, we do so in a way that infers immediate negative consequence.

There are different kinds or levels of fear: primal, justified fear (survival, self-preservation) and fears imposed by society, parents, religion, and so on, that have more to do with shame, guilt, and other non-lethal or immediate threats.

In some cases, a person's fear is based on a stimulus that is immediate and of significant adverse consequence, linked to self-preservation. For example, if a person encountered a rattlesnake, it would make sense that he or she would experience an *immediate* fear. A person's fear in this particular example alerts the person who the snake is dangerous and that he or she must avoid getting bitten to stay alive or at least free of pain.

There are other times in which a person feels fear without necessarily understanding why or being able to pinpoint the source of the fear. This can be described as an *indirect* fear. An indirect fear does not require an immediate action for the purpose of self-preservation. However, in many instances, indirect fears do affect a person's decision-making processes in conjunction with any number of socially imposed expectations to conform to the status quo.

Fear as a catalyst can prompt a person to take action in the direction of his or her goals. Decisions made along the way to a lofty goal—such as acceptance into a prestigious university, being hired for a coveted position, or building a house—may be rooted in fear: fear of hard work, fear of a demanding commitment of time or money, fear of not having enough knowledge to accomplish the necessary tasks, and so on.

Internal fears also arise: "Am I good enough?" "Am I smart enough?" "Am I strong enough?" "What do I need to give up to accomplish my goal?" "What if I fail?" "What if so-and-so doesn't like me?" The list of self-talk can go on and on.

The key, I believe, to achieving one's goals—lofty or not—is learning to recognize the fears that stand in our way, then to manage or even embrace those fears, and then move forward, rather than being paralyzed into non-action or even giving up on the goals.

I encourage you to take a moment to reflect on your own successes and failures. In almost all cases, I would be willing to bet that your end results could be traced to whether or not you were able to manage your fear, or you allowed your fear to manage you.

The METUS Principle was developed to help you and others learn to **recognize** fear in its many disguises, to better **understand** the source of those fears, and then to **manage** those fears in ourselves and others. The intent is to help you successfully move forward in your life and maximize your potential.

Whether you are a business leader, a politician a student, a parent, or fulfilling myriad other roles— recognizing, understanding, and managing your fear will bring you closer to realizing your goals.

To your success,

Brian A. Peters

Chapter One

Psychology and Fear

Maria's Story:
Survivor from the 83rd Floor

When they were completed and opened in 1973, the "Twin Towers" of the World Trade Center Complex, in New York City, were the tallest buildings in the world, each standing 110 floors high. Within twelve years, the World Trade Center Complex would see five additional buildings constructed for a total of seven. Each day, nearly 150,000 people used the World Trade subway stations, 50,000 of whom worked in the Twin Towers. Every day, employees would shuffle aboard express elevators that would carry them quickly up and down each building at speeds up to 19 mph. Those working on floors 1 to 78 boarded an express elevator and got off at their floors. Those who worked in offices above floor 78 had to take an express elevator to 78 and then hop on local elevators to get to higher floors.

Maria was one of the 50,000 people who worked in the World Trade Center's Twin Towers. Earning her bachelor's degree in Industrial Engineering and her M.B.A. in finance from NYU, Maria secured a position working as a business analyst and project manager for the Port Authority of New York and New Jersey. In 2001, as a member of the Port Authority, Maria worked on the 86th floor of Tower 1 and was responsible for replacing a twelve-year-old computer system in the building.

Her commute each morning started in New Jersey, where she boarded a Central New Jersey train to Newark. Making a connection in Newark, she would board another train that would take her to a station right below the Towers. By her own account, the security measures for passengers in and out of tower station were impressive. She recalled a statement she made to a friend, about a week prior to the 9/11 attacks: "The towers really are secure from the bottom up—but what is to stop a helicopter from dropping a bomb on them?"

Those who had been involved in the 1993 World Trade Center bombing, or more familiar with the event, could not help but consider and appreciate the level of security required to manage the flow of 50,000 employees and another 100,000 or more visitors each day. But like Maria, many employees realized that no security measures were impenetrable or absolute.

On September 11, 2001, as Maria made her way off the local elevators onto the 83rd floor, she noticed smoke and fire coming from the opposite elevator on the same floor. Quickly, she made her way to a nearby business office in an effort to call building security to alert them of the problem. As she attempted her call, she heard a man say, "A plane hit the building – a big one!"

Despite his comments, Maria remained calm; the man became nearly frozen at that point. While on the phone, she remembered looking out of the windows and seeing papers floating around everywhere. It was at that moment she decided to call her husband, let him know that she was okay, and that she was waiting for a rescue team.

While waiting, Maria caught a glimpse of Tower 2. She could see red and orange flames and it was at that moment she was certain, "This was not an accident!" While still attempting to remain calm, Maria looked around at the others and told them, "We need to get out of here." It was at that moment others around her started to panic. She recalled a statement made by a young man nearest her, "This can't be happening. I just had a baby."

As they attempted to make their way to a set of stairs, reality started to really hit home. The air was a thick, foggy soup. Through the murky air, she could see a light, and she heard a voice, "How many of you are there?" asked the voice.

"About eight," she responded.

"Come with me."

Following the voice, Maria and her seven compan- ions made their way through the fog to a staircase that was already crowded with people. Maria remembers hearing a lot of cursing and fear from those making their way down —especially from those who had been through the '93 bombing.

As thousands of employees made their way down the stairs, Maria remembers fire crews and emergency responders racing up. As she made her way down, she recalled how wet it was, and at first, she thought the wetness was a good thing. She assumed the sprinklers were dousing the fire, which is why it was so wet everywhere. However, she later learned the moisture was because one of the planes hitting the towers and destroying the plumbing pipes. The water needed to fight the fire never made it to where it needed to go.

While racing down the stairs, Maria remembered seeing several young people turn around or make their way back to their offices as they muttered that the staircases were "too crowded." Going as quickly as possible, she soon caught up to her supervisor, Jean. Maria knew that Jean had a heart condition and a pacemaker, and recognized that the strenuous activity, as well as the stressful nature of the situation, were not good for her superior.

Rather than pass her by, Maria walked with and supported Jean as they made their way down the staircase together. Maria was concerned for her own safety, and knew that she needed to get out of the building as quickly as possible, but she could not leave Jean. Together, they noticed all the damage that had occurred. From an engineering standpoint, Maria observed that the walls were longer standing at right angles; the escalators they could see were twisting themselves into pretzels, and other structural elements of the building were noticeably disfigured.

Around the 5th, 6th, or 7th floor, she remembers a huge rumble. It felt like nothing less than an earthquake. While neither she nor Jean knew it at the time, the tremendous quake was in fact Tower 2 coming down! At that moment, the safest place for them to be was near floor 5 in Tower 1...right where they were.

Many of those fleeing passed Maria and Jean in the staircase. The two women made it out just in time to see the neighboring tower fall on top of those who had "escaped."

In recounting this story, Maria told me, "While Jean has thanked me many times for staying with her and for saving her life, I know it was Jean who actually saved mine." Maria said that Jean had slowed her down just enough to avoid the falling tower while making it out of Tower 1 with but ten minutes to spare before their own tower collapsed and suffered the same fate.

As the two of them exited their tower, she recalls rescuers yelling, "Don't look up! Don't look back!" Instead, they were directed to make their way quickly away from the Towers and up the street. However, Maria's curiosity, and the intensity of the moment, caused her to pause a moment to look back. When she saw the other building, as well as her own, she knew, "This is Major-League bad, and this was intentional."

For the first time, Maria started to feel a deep sense of worry and concern. "Is this going to be the beginning of World War III?" she wondered. And if the devastation of the Towers was not bad enough, she couldn't help but wonder what other violence would be cast upon the city and those trying to escape with their lives?

Now that she was safely out and away from the tower, she wondered about biological and chemical weapons; a thought that would keep her away from any water in the city as she attempted to make her way home. She realized, as bad as the Towers were, and as much devastation that has already occurred, this could be only the beginning.

As she began talking about her journey back home, she recalled walking the streets. In her words, "I was a complete mess. You have seen the pictures, right? I pretty much looked like that. But you know what? New York comes together in an emergency unlike any other city. As we walked, we could already see signs up for blood donations to help victims. We saw thousands of New Yorkers rushing toward the Towers to help." She saw the Inn on 48th taking in survivors, offering them food, giving them a place to get cleaned up and make phone calls to loved ones.

Marie had to rely on a cab to get home. She remembers getting into the cab wondering, "What if a bomb goes off while we are on the George Washington Bridge?" While in the cab crossing the bridge, she recalls holding hands tightly with a woman she rode with. Together they were both hoping, with every fiber of their being, that a bomb would not go off while they were on the bridge.

When she got out of the cab at the train station in Newark, she looked around at all the cars in the parking lot. A surreal feeling came over her as she realized, "Some people will not be coming back to pick up their cars tonight."

In the days following the attacks, Marie watched the news almost continuously. She wanted to learn more. Who had done these terrible things? Why had they done it? And, what was happening to prevent any additional violence against American citizens?

As a result of the attacks, Maria no longer works in New York City. She now has a job on the 2nd floor in a New Jersey office and avoids taking public transit. She is not shy about acknowledging that the attacks of 9/11 changed her. She believes the attacks have made a lasting impression on her in many ways –particularly as related to fear. She believes the attacks of 9/11 have made her more aware of her surroundings, each and every day. In her mind, she is constantly thinking, "What if....?" And she believes it is important for people to "always have a plan."

Marie has also recognized and learned to understand her potential fear. She said, "We are not out of the woods. With every day that goes by, it seems that people lose sight of what was done [to us]; and that is a dangerous thing. I don't believe we are properly funding programs to prevent such attacks from happening again. It is only a matter of time."

Given what Maria went through, and her amazing story of survival, I asked her what major lessons she has learned about fear. How does she manage it? The first thing she said was that in order to manage fear, you have to somehow manage to stay calm. You have to be able to assess your surroundings and make informed decisions about what you need to not only do now, but what you also need to do next.

As she recounted, she immediately began citing examples. "The people I remember, and who I would want to be around in the time of crisis, were not the young and the strong. Those people panicked and I saw them make some very bad choices. The people I would want to be around are older gentlemen with military experience. They kept calm and proceeded to do what they needed to do."

I asked her if there was anything else she thought was important to know about fear. Very concisely, she said, "It is okay to be afraid...as long as you can stay calm and do what you need to do. That is how you get through a crisis and that is how you survive."

* * * * *

If you plan on being anything less than you are capable of being, you will probably be unhappy all the days of your life.
—Abraham Maslow

A failure is not always a mistake, it may simply be the best one can do under the circumstances. The real mistake is to stop trying.
—B. F. Skinner

Psychology, or the study of the psyche, the mind, has four general goals: 1) describe what has occurred, 2) explain why it has occurred, 3) predict what will occur, and 4) control how to make something occur. Within this field there are four modern perspectives: psychoanalytic, behavioral, cognitive, and ecological theories. The following provides a brief explanation of each theory and explains how fear can serve as a substitute for, or complement, key assumptions of each.

PSYCHOANALYTIC THEORIES

Psychoanalytic theorists, such as Sigmund Freud (Austrian, 1856-1939) and Carl Jung (Swiss, 1875-1961) believed that human behavior is deterministic, meaning that behavior is governed by irrational forces and the unconscious, as well instinctual and biological drives. Because of the deterministic nature of behavior, psychoanalytic theorists do not believe in free will.

Perhaps the most famous of psychoanalytic theorists is Sigmund Freud, considered the father of modern psychoanalysis. Freud determined that the personality consists of three different elements: the Id, the Ego and the Superego.

According to Freud , the Id is the aspect of personality driven by internal and basic drives and needs. These are typically instinctual, such as hunger, thirst, and the drive for sex, or libido. The Id acts in accordance with the pleasure principle, in that it avoids pain and seeks pleasure. Today, this behavior is often described as the notion of instant gratification. Due to the instinctual quality of the Id, it is impulsive and often unaware of the implications of actions taken.

The Superego is driven by morality. The Superego acts in connection with the morality of higher thought and action. Instead of instinctually acting like the Id, the Superego works to act in socially acceptable ways. It employs morality, the sense of wrong and right, and uses guilt to encourage socially acceptable behavior. Oftentimes, the Superego operates under a deeper desire for delayed gratification.

The Ego is driven by reality. The Ego works to balance both the Id's immediate desires and the Superego's long-term goals. To balance these two opposing forces, the Ego generally works to achieve the Id's drive in the most realistic ways. It seeks to rationalize the Id's instinct and please the drives that will benefit the individual in the long term. It helps distinguish what is real and realistic in our drives, as well as being realistic about the standards the Superego sets for the individual.

The Ego balances the Id, the Superego, and reality to maintain an individual's healthy state of consciousness. It thus reacts to protect the individual from any stressors and anxiety by distorting reality, if necessary. This prevents threatening unconscious thoughts and material from entering the consciousness. The different types of defense mechanisms used by the Ego are: repression, reaction formation, denial, projection, displacement, sublimation, regression, and rationalization.

Now, let's use Freud's classic framework that incorporates the concept of fear. While I agree with Freud's account of basic drive and motivating forces, I believe he had pleasure and pain reversed and that even more fundamental than pain is fear. For example, when a baby is born its first instinct is to cry. I am convinced that a baby cries out of fear—primarily fear of the unknown. A mother can respond to her baby's cry by immediately comforting the child, commonly through nursing.

I experienced this phenomenon first-hand when my daughter, Kensington, was born. As soon as she was delivered, my wife nursed her and comforted her, which reduced her fears of being in a new environment. I contend that a baby's first response to the world is fearful. When it experiences something pleasurable—a warm caress, hearing the mother's heartbeat—that fear is lessened or quelled.

Unlike Freud, I do not believe that pain is the lowest common denominator in human behavior. We can reduce that which is painful to that which we fear. Greek philosopher Aristotle referred to this relationship as that which has *potential* versus that which is *actual*. A person's pain is something he or she experiences in the moment. A person's fear is the realization that something bad, i.e. something that causes pain, could potentially harm the individual. A person's actual fear is the result of that individual's expectation of pain. Fear thus precedes pain and becomes the lowest common denominator and something a person attempts to avoid.

In the process of avoiding fear, we seek pleasure. That which is pleasurable reduces our fear. Again, I will refer back to a newborn baby. Nursing is both nourishing and comforting. Receiving nourishment and comfort is pleasurable, which is why they both reduce fear. Nourishment addresses a physiological need, while comfort addresses a natural need for safety, love, and belonging.

* * * * *

Freud's Superego is driven by morality. The Superego acts in conjunction with the morality of higher thought and action. In essence, the Superego is the long-term projection of who and what individuals want to "be." The Superego is a projection of one's ideal self. When a person considers social norms, morality concept, and value judgments, the Superego demonstrates who a person could be when he or she learns to recognize, understand, and manage fear. The Superego is thus a projection of one's self-actualized self.

Now, consider the Ego. The Ego is driven by reality. It serves to achieve the Id's drive for instant gratification in the most realistic ways, while at the same time considering the Superego's image of one's ideal self. The Ego is constantly balancing what a person may have immediately to satisfy the Id's wants versus what the person's Superego strives to become. I contend that this is a relationship that pits causal and corollary decision-making against one another.

To better understand this balance, consider the following. A high school teenager may have an important English paper due on Monday. It also happens that there is a huge party on the weekend prior to the paper being due. The student needs at least a B+ to earn an overall A for the course and keep his GPA near the top of the class.

What is this particular student more afraid of? Is he more afraid of missing the party or more afraid of turning in a poor paper and running the risk of harming his grade point average? If the teen is more afraid of missing the party and risking social embarrassment/anger of his girlfriend, he will likely decide to put off writing the paper, or rush through it to get it done before the party.

Whether he puts the assignment off until after the party or rushes to get it done before the party, the student is aware that his choice likely means that he will be giving less than his best effort. If the student decides he is willing to turn in a paper that is less than his best effort in favor of attending the party, he is addressing his immediate fear, which is missing the party. On Maslow's hierarchy, this is related to both belonging and esteem, and demonstrates causal thinking behavior.

On the other hand, if the student decides to forego the party because he is more afraid of turning in a poor paper, he is demonstrating that he is more afraid of harming his GPA than he is of missing the party. This requires corollary thinking, which moves into the future beyond the actual moment.

The student had to make a choice between going to a party and working on an important school assignment. Attending the party would be the preference of the Id, as this would provide instant gratification. Foregoing the party to work on a school assignment would be the preference of the Superego, because this course of action requires sacrifice and delaying gratification to move closer to achieving what the Superego hopes to become.

The student's decision, to attend or forego the party, is fundamentally rooted in fear. Is the student more afraid of missing out on a chance for instant gratification, which is the party, or is he more afraid of turning in a poorly prepared assignment, and possibly harming his chances of gaining acceptance into a desired college? The choice here becomes one of causation (short-term) and correlation (long-term).

We can attribute pleasure, in a direct sense, to attending the party. In other words, attending the party is a causal relation to the student's pleasure experience. The homework assignment, in this example, is corollary. It does not directly impact the goal of the Superego, and as such, is only one of a number of variable factors that impact the student's chances of getting into his desired school. If the student opted to forego the party, worked hard, and received an 'A' on the assignment, that factor would not be the cause of the student's gaining acceptance into the school of his choice, just as getting a grade lower than an 'A' would not necessarily result in his being rejected by that school.

The fundamental questions in this decision-making scenario are: What is the student more afraid of and how will he manage his fear? Will he allow his Id and immediate fear guide his action(s) or will he focus on his long-term fear and act in accordance with the desires of his Superego?

Managing short-term versus long-term fears is often one of the most difficult challenges a person can face. It is often much easier to give into short-term desires because causal relationships are easier for people to understand or rationalize than corollary ones to which there is no direct relationship. If a person's Ego is able to properly understand and manage his or her fears, a person is able to maintain a healthier life balance and act in a way that will help maximize opportunities, both short-term and long-term.

BEHAVIORAL THEORIES

B.F. Skinner (American, 1904–1990) was a firm believer that the concept of free will did not exist in human beings, and that any action or behavior was based on consequences of that action. If the consequences were bad, it was likely the action would not be repeated. However, if the results of the action were positive, those actions could be reinforced. Skinner developed his own philosophy of science called radical behaviorism, and founded his own school of psychology, called the experimental analysis of behavior, or EAB.

EAB differs from other approaches to behavioral research in that Skinner's radical behaviorism accepts feelings, states of mind, and introspection as existent and scientifically treatable. However, radical behaviorism stops short of identifying feelings as causes of behavior.

It is, in my opinion, unfortunate that many behaviorists decided not to identify feelings as causes for behavior. Had Skinner attempted to take his work one step farther, and attempt to identify and understand feelings as causes of behavior, he might have discovered that fear is the fundamental drive and cause of human behavior. Our behavior is an effort to avoid things that cause us fear or take action to overcome that fear. My belief is that all actions a person takes are fundamentally rooted in fear.

To understand this notion, we cannot look at fear in its most traditional sense. Instead, we must consider fear as a fundamental drive or catalyst. For example, I may ask someone, "Why do you eat?"

The person's response might be, "Because I like food."

To which I would ask, "Why do you like food?"

The person might say, "Because I am hungry, and when I eat, I am no longer hungry."

Then I would ask, "Why do you want to satisfy your hunger?"

This question-and-answer process could go on for a while. At some point, the person will realize that if he did not eat, he would ultimately die. We need nourishment to survive. Thus the need to eat is part of our natural drive for self-preservation, a survival instinct, which at its most fundamental level is rooted in fear.

COGNITIVE THEORIES

The theory of cognitive development is a comprehensive theory about the nature and development of human intelligence, first developed by Jean Piaget (1896 – 1980), a Swiss developmental psychologist and philosopher. It is primarily known as a developmental stage theory, but in fact, it deals with the nature of knowledge itself and how humans come to gradually acquire, construct, and use it.

To Piaget, cognitive development was a progressive reorganization of mental processes as a result of biological maturation and environmental experience. Children construct an understanding of the world around them, and then experience discrepancies between what they already know and what they discover in their environment. Piaget claims the idea that cognitive development is at the center of the human organism and language is contingent on cognitive development. Piaget believed that reality is a dynamic system of continuous change, and as such, is defined in reference to the two conditions that establish dynamic systems: transformation and state.

Transformation refers to all manners of changes a thing or person can undergo. *State* refers to the conditions or the appearances in which things or persons can be found between transformations. For example, there might be changes in shape or form (for instance, liquids are reshaped as they are transferred from one vessel to another; humans change in their characteristics as they grow older), in size (e.g., a series of coins on a table might be placed close to each other or farther apart), or in placement or location in space and time (e.g., various objects or persons might be found at one place at one time and at a different place at another time).

Piaget theorized that if human intelligence is to be adaptive, it must have functions to represent both the transformational and the static aspects of reality. He proposed that operative intelligence is responsible for the representation and manipulation of the dynamic or transformational aspects of reality and that figurative intelligence is responsible for the representation of the static aspects of reality.

I agree with Piaget. I believe that as people grow, develop, and have different environmental experiences, they learn to manage their fears. They learn to recognize what they should avoid or could harm them. They also learn what they are attracted to or that which they find pleasurable.

Of the two possible options offered by Piaget—transformation and state—the concept of fear can readily be applied to both, because we naturally fear the unknown, and until we have an experience, we cannot move past our natural inclination to fear it. Children come to understand the world around them through experiences. I believe that cognitive development, at its most fundamental level, is the ongoing process of managing fear. Our ability to navigate through life and make choices is a dynamic system of continuous change. The choices we make reflect our experiences and are shaped by our fears being confirmed or subdued.

Piaget also recognized that if human intelligence is to be adaptive, it must have functions to represent both the transformational and static aspects of reality, in other words, that which "is" and that which may "become." This concept is rooted in Greek tradition and describes that which is actual and that which is potential. With respect to fear, this may be described as "that which we fear" and "that which we are afraid of."

Our fear is general and what we *are afraid of* is more specific. One of the simplest examples I can offer is bodily harm. Bodily harm would be the general fear; an individual would be afraid of anything perceived that could cause bodily harm. Most people are afraid of tigers and would fear bodily harm if they were inside a cage with a tiger. There are some who work with the magnificent beasts on a regular basis, however, and while they fear bodily harm, because of their experience as trainers, they may not be afraid of the tigers.

As another example, most people fear darkness. I contend that it is not the darkness *per se* that they are afraid of, as darkness in and of itself cannot hurt or cause bodily harm. Rather, people are afraid of all the things that might be lurking in the darkness—the mugger, the steep stairway, the unknown.

At the center of Piaget's theory of cognitive development is a progressive reorganization of mental processes that result from biological maturation and environmental experience. As a result, human intelligence is adaptive, transformational, and what is known at a given moment is representative of all that people have come to know: our reality.

To illustrate my point, I will attempt to do so through the lens of Western vs. Middle Eastern relations. Both sides are committed to their respective position(s), which are rooted in religion and various philosophical beliefs. Over the centuries, the differences in traditions, values, and customs between Christians and Muslims have guided the actions of people within the two belief systems. In many occasions, actions taken by each of the two sides have been interpreted as hostile and aggressive by the other—which has increased the levels of distrust and fear between the two sides. Over time, and as a result of a combination of real and perceived negative experiences, Christians and Muslims have learned to fear one another. It could also be argued that as a matter of security and self -preservation, they remain at odds and lack trust with one another. How each party interprets its environment and the relationships within its environment, impacts how it manages fear, which serves as the basis of its action(s).

ECOLOGICAL THEORY

Urie Bronfenbrenner (1917–2005) was a Russian American psychologist who is regarded as one of the world's leading scholars in the field of developmental psychology. His Ecological Systems Theory holds that human development reflects the influence of several environmental systems. It identifies five environmental systems with which an individual interacts. His work is particularly important because it helps illustrate the relationship to fear as being both innate and learned, based on developmental and experiential processes. Our innate, inborn fear is either confirmed by our experiences, or it is mitigated by them, within each of his five systems:

- A *microsystem* refers to the institutions and groups that most immediately and directly impact a child's development, including family, school, religious institutions, neighborhood, and peers.

- A *mesosystem* refers to relations between microsystems or connections between contexts. Examples are the relation of family experiences to school experiences, school experiences to church experiences, and family experiences to peer experiences. For example, children whose parents have rejected them may have difficulty developing positive relations with teachers.

- The *exosystem* involves links between a social setting in which the individual does not have an active role and the individual's immediate context.

For example, a husband or child's experience at home may be influenced by a mother's experiences at work. The mother might receive a promotion that requires more travel, which might increase conflict with the husband and change patterns of interaction with the child.

- The *macrosystem* describes the culture in which individuals live. Cultural contexts include growing up in a developing or industrialized country, socioeconomic status, poverty, and ethnicity. A child, his or her parents, his or her school, and his or her parent's workplace are all part of a large cultural context. Members of a cultural group share a common identity, heritage, and values. The macrosystem evolves over time, because each successive generation may change the macrosystem, leading to its development in a unique macrosystem.

- The *chronosystem* is the patterning of environmental events and transitions over an individual's life course, as well as socio-historical circumstances. For example, divorces are one transition. Researchers have found that the negative effects of divorce on children often peak in the first year after the divorce. By two years after the divorce, family interaction is less chaotic and more stable. An example of socio-historical circumstances is the increase in opportunities for women to pursue a career during the last thirty years.

Bronfrenbrenner's work in the area of ecological systems, in my opinion, can be seen as one of the better ways to illustrate how people learn to recognize and manage their fears. I also like his work because it helps identify fear in terms of an individual's specific interactions and environment. People will not all maintain the same degree of fear, at all times, and in all scenarios, because each individual's experiences help shape how he or she responds.

For example, the *microsystem* provides people with, or can take away from, their sense of safety. What people fear, regardless of age, and to what extent, depends on how safe they feel in their immediate environment.

The *mesosystem* speaks to a person's sense of love and belonging. If a person is not accepted or provided with a sense of security, it is possible that a persistent fear or anxiety could appear in other relationships.

The *exosystem* involves links between a social setting in which the individual does not have an active role and the individual's immediate context. These relationships can impact a person's self-esteem. A child will pick up on interactions and decisions made around them. Depending on how they perceive particular actions, and what they attribute the actions to, people may develop a particular fear based on something they did not experience directly, or experienced directly but only marginally.

The *macrosystem* describes the culture in which individuals live. Environmental factors contribute significantly to a person's ability to progress toward self-actualization. If basic needs are not met, a person will be unable, or at best, will have significant difficulty, to move beyond them to address more complex opportunities.

For example, in poorer communities, many people find it difficult to meet even the most basic human needs: food, water, clothing, shelter. They will struggle with doing enough to survive, and as a result, very little attention or consideration is given to the future. Under such environmental conditions, these people are victims of their macrosystem. Until they are able to meet those basic needs, they will not progress up Maslow's pyramid. It is likely that generational fear is present—that is, the fears of one's ancestors, grandparents, and parents will remain the same over time, and be incorporated into the culture's traditions and social norms.

Finally, the *chronosystem* is the patterning of environmental events and transitions over the life course, as well as socio-historical circumstances. The chronosystem is a person's state-of-being in motion either closer to, or further from, realizing self-actualization.

Abraham Maslow (1908-1970), offered his Hierarchy of Needs in *A Theory of Human Motivation*, written in 1943, which states that psychological health is predicated on fulfilling innate human needs, from safety and shelter, and culminating in self-actualization. The levels coincide quite well with those of the previous discussion and the image below provides an outstanding visual for helping people understand how people operationalize fear and progress from the simple to the complex.

Maslow's hierarchy can be utilized to explain fear in relation to human behavior. Over time and across disciplines, I began to see Maslow's hierarchy for what it truly is: a journey toward mastering one's fears. At the bottom of his pyramid illustration, he offers primitive survival needs. As we advance from lower tiers to higher tiers, we develop a greater sense of security. This is an inverse relationship: less security, more fear; more security, less fear. At the apex is the point of self-actualization, at which a person has mastered fear and is no longer limited by it. If Maslow were to make the connection between one's quest for true security by successfully managing one's own fear, he could have just as easily called it, *A Theory of Fear.*

Most people feel discomfort or pain, but don't realize their response is based on fear—which can be fear of humiliation, rejection, failure, and so on. If a person does not recognize fear, it is difficult to manage it. Knowing that you're afraid and recognizing what you are afraid of are huge steps toward managing fear.

MASLOW'S HIERARCHY OF NEEDS

Let's look again at the METUS image below. As discussed in the Preface, anchoring the image is a pyramid, inspired by the work of Abraham Maslow. I have modified his Pyramid of Human Needs to better illustrate the role fear plays throughout our lives in our pursuit of self-actualization. The yin and yang symbol embedded in the pyramid reflect the opposite, yet interconnected, forces in our lives.

The two smaller pyramids, one pointing up, the other down, illustrate the dynamism of our ever-changing lives. We are in a constant state of transition based on our experiences and the world around us. Just because we have achieved a modicum of success and have been able to move closer toward our actualized self, does not mean

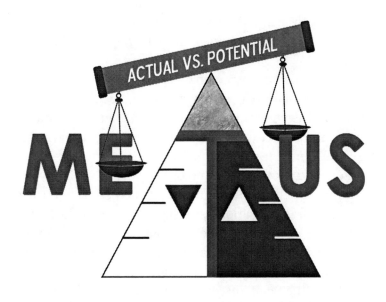

we will remain there. To do so requires work on our end, and further advancement means even more work.

We can go up or down the pyramid continuum, both by our own effort and due to our environment. As we move up or down, what we are afraid of may change, but fear will not. Fear will always be there because it's part of the human experience. It is important that we recognize, understand, and manage our fear, so that we can determine where to focus our time, attention, energy, and other resources to be able to achieve our goal of self-actualization.

SUMMARY

Because psychology aims to explain why people are who they are and why they do what they do, an entire book could be written outlining in great specificity how fear might serve as the basis for each of the four psychological schools of thought. However, my purpose is to illustrate how the notion of fear does, in fact, transcend time and place.

If the goal of psychology is to describe what has occurred, explain why it has occurred, predict what will occur, and control future occurrences, then understanding what a person fears and how he or she manages that fear, is essential to understanding human behavior.

Fear and success are interconnected, and certainly not everyone has the same definition of success. The journey toward self-actualization is a personal, individual, and deep endeavor. Every fiber of our being is a unique combination of biological and environmental conditions that make us who we are. It is not up to me, or anyone else, to define what success means to you. Only you can do that. And one of the intentions of this book is to help you better understand who you want to be and help you develop an awareness of how to achieve your goals.

While we are different in so many ways, there is one commonality – the very essence of the human experience – we are all born with the capacity to fear.

Given that we are all imbued with fear, it is important that we learn to embrace it and learn how and why it is a catalyst for behavior; both our own fear and the fear of others. Once we are able to embrace fear as a natural phenomenon, recognize our fear, understand fear within the context of our lives, then we will be able to manage our fear in a way that allows us to progress toward our own individual concepts of success.

Fear is not to be feared, but rather to be understood. People are often afraid and reluctant to even identify their fears because they view fear as a sign of weakness. To accept that we are afraid is not a sign of weakness, but rather, a sign of strength. It takes courage to recognize our fear, understand our fear, and manage our fear. If self -actualization is the treasure chest and fear is the lock, then the METUS Principle is the key!

NOTES

CHAPTER TWO
PHILOSOPHY AND FEAR

Linda Braun's story:
President of Braun Marketing Group

She was the Director of Group Sales for the Ritz-Carlton Hotel New York, Battery Park. The hotel had not yet opened; it was scheduled to do so in October. The only people in the property were administrative and management staff.

On the morning of 9/11, she arrived at work just before the first plane hit the first of the Twin Towers of the World Trade Center. While sitting at her desk, a co-worker's friend called to tell them that the WTC was on fire. All of the administrative offices were in the basement, so Linda and others decided to walk upstairs and outside to see what was happening.

The hotel was located approximately five blocks from the WTC, and the WTC literally towered over them. When they walked outside and looked up, they could immediately see that the Tower was on fire, but, the first plane had entered from the North, so they could not see the extent of damage from their angle. Horrified, Linda and her co-workers stared at the fire. She assumed the fire department would be able to put it out and went back down to her office with her co-workers.

When the second plane hit, she felt and heard a loud and distinct thump. She had no idea what it was and didn't react to it. Minutes later, the organization's Chief Engineer ran down to their offices, banged loudly on the emergency exit doors, and screamed, "Get Out, Get Out!" Instantaneously, the fire alarms throughout the building started screaming. Linda yelled "grab your purses" to her coworkers and staff and everyone raced through the emergency exit door and upstairs.

When they emerged from the building, they looked to the Towers and immediately could see what had happened. The second plane had come in from the south, so they could see the extent of the damage from their direction.

It was unbelievable. There was a clear impact spot on the second tower with smoke and flames shooting everywhere. The first impact's damage was now much more visible, with what appeared to be an entire section of the Tower in flames on all sides.

Linda could not process what was happening and ran to a friend of hers who was closer to the street. She told Linda she had been walking out of the subway and the second plane buzzed right over her on the way to the Tower. It appeared to have almost clipped our building, as theirs was the tallest structure coming from that direction. Linda's friend had immediately called her producer friends at the *Today Show* and they had put her live on the air to describe what she was seeing. (She had previously worked at the *Today Show* in production.)

As Linda looked around, people were running in every direction, gathering in groups, and all were staring at the Towers in disbelief. One of her coworkers, who happened to be a Vietnam veteran, said it was terrorists who had hijacked the planes and flew them into the Towers. Linda thought he was crazy and likely paranoid. A woman who worked at their sister hotel in the World Trade Center had run so fast from the scene, she had sprained an ankle and was hobbling around as people were helping her. The look she had on her face was indescribable.

People were gathering in small groups to account for everyone. And they were all staring up at the Towers. It was the oddest feeling – utterly surreal.

The situation at WTC was obviously getting worse. They kept seeing paper flying out of the windows, tiny specs, and then we realized there were larger shapes as well – people falling from the WTC. Linda couldn't watch and had to look away; she urged others to look away as well. It seemed somehow disrespectful to the people who were falling.

For Linda, it was time to get out of the area. All she wanted to do was get home. She didn't know if it was safer, but she knew it wasn't there. She informed her superiors the she was leaving. They didn't want her to go, but she didn't care. They were not responsible for her and she could make her own choices. Most people wanted to stay and continue observing, but a small group of her coworkers wanted to leave as well. They decided to walk up the east side – on the west side was the World

Financial Center and they didn't know what was happening there.

They started walking—five women in high heels – and continued walking for three straight hours on city streets. They were all numb and at some level of shock. Linda couldn't reach her husband because her cell phone wouldn't work. One of her friend's phone was functioning but Linda couldn't remember her husband's number because it was on speed dial in her phone. To this day, she repeats his cell phone number in her head to ensure she remembers it if she need to call without speed dial.

During their trek, Linda and her co-workers were joined by thousands all going in the same direction. They got news along the way by people shouting it to each other and cab drivers stopped in the streets with their windows open and their radios at full volume. They heard the Pentagon had been hit, the White House – maybe. the Statue of Liberty was a target. There was a lot of misinformation and confusion.

They saw fighter jets flying above us and it scared us to death. They passed a homeless man sitting on a bench without a care in the world and a smile on his face, watching thousands of people in a panic going by him. Linda's PTSD therapist later told me it was because he felt he had nothing to lose, so why run away?

At one point, the crowd started to surge and run. The women looked back and started running as well, until someone in the crowd yelled authoritatively "Slow the F$#K down" and everyone actually, did which diffused an immediate danger of trampling. In consideration, Linda is sure that's when the Tower fell. By that time, they were far enough ahead that they never got hit by the dust and debris.

Eventually, Linda made it to E. 59th. Her co-workers had all split off to get to their apartments and she just needed to walk straight west on 59th to get to hers.

As she walked up Central Park South, she passed a TV studio with a wall of TV screens. A huge crowd of people was gathered watching the coverage. They were crying and clearly in disbelief. Linda finally made it to her apartment building and told the doorman where she had been. The street was blocked off because there was a hospital next door and they closed the traffic down to get ready for the ambulances – which ultimately never came as there were not enough survivors.

As Linda entered her building, a group of very macho guys ran up to the doorman to ask where they could give blood; they knew there was a hospital nearby. They were doing the one thing they knew they could do to help.

Linda made it up to her apartment and collapsed.

* * * * *

True wisdom comes to each of us when we realize how little we understand about life, ourselves, and the world around us.
—Socrates

*For a man to conquer himself
is the first and noblest of all victories.*
—Plato

The goal of philosophy is to aspire to a universal truth and produce propositions that would be acceptable to any rational person anywhere at any time. According to the Greek philosopher, Plato, enlightened people understand just how much they don't know and how ignorant they truly are. It is for this very reason that Socrates died trying to get people to "know themselves."

There is a continuum of philosophical theory that includes the works of a wide array of influential thinkers. One of my greatest challenges was deciding to which theories and theorists I should devote the most time. Of course, I started with the Greeks, as they are considered by many to be the originators of philosophy as we have come to know it.

Within each of the four philosophical perspectives exists the notion of fear. Depending on the specific philosophy and how it is applied to practical examples, the concept of fear may be discussed slightly differently.

Once I moved beyond Socrates, Plato, and Aristotle, I found myself concentrating on the most notable philosophical theories and less on individual philosophers; with a few exceptions. Following is a brief explanation of each theory and explanation of the ways fear can substitute or complement the key assumptions of each.

I have found myself drawn to different philosophical theories at various times, because I believe every one of them possesses grains of truth. I have also come to realize that the position's philosophers take provide a window into their lives, their individual experiences, and how each has come to explain the world around him. As a result, I believe that most theories can explain, at least in part, the conditions of human existence, which is precisely their intent.

A person's state of mind and personal experiences will also determine which theorists and theories to which that person is most attracted. Individuals who are new to philosophy and do not become fixated on one particular perspective may change their perspectives over time. This has certainly been the case for me, especially as I have crossed into different academic concentrations and viewed them through multiple academic and professional lenses.

Four major philosophical perspectives have considerably influenced modern Western society and our views in the United States: Idealism, Realism, Pragmatism, and Existentialism. Each of the four perspectives reflects the period in which they were created and thus embeds the societal values of that era. Below, I will address how each perspective is impacted by the concept of fear, and how fear plays a role in our lives.

IDEALISM

Representatives of this perspective include Plato, Immanuel Kant, Georg Hegel, and Arthur Schopenhauer. A primary goal for a philosophical idealist is discovering higher levels of understanding.

Idealism is one the oldest of the four schools of philosophical thought and is grounded in the desire to discover absolute or universal truth. Plato, a Greek philosopher (428-347 BC) believed that because the world around us is constantly changing, only the world of ideas is "real," or absolute truth. Whenever we see something in our mind's eye or experience fear in our thoughts, we are creating our environment in the world of ideas, rather than in the physical world.

More recent idealists, such as Immanuel Kant (1724-1804) and Georg Hegel (1770-1831), have focused on the process of reasoning, intuition, and religious revelation, and they have downplayed any emphasis on a singular truth. For example, Kant believed it possible to achieve moral clarification, but not to arrive at an absolute or universal truth. Hegel, on the other hand, thought that one could progress toward truth by continually analyzing ideas, aiming to support or refute what had previously been presented by others.

Consider Immanuel Kant's position as an idealist. Kant synthesized early modern rationalism and empiricism, believed it possible to achieve moral clarification, but not possible to arrive at an absolute or universal truth.

Now, let's apply this principle to the concept of fear. Based on Kant's perspective, each individual will know fear and experience fear differently. How a person internalizes his fear, based on his own experiences and recognition of that fear, understanding of that fear, and personal management of that fear, will be as real to the person as any physical force in the universe.

That is not to say, however, that a particular fear is universal. For example, what you fear and what I fear may be completely different because our life experiences and our environment. Nonetheless, your fear is no less real to you than mine is to me. Thus, the moral clarification of our fears can be realized, but the universality of our fears cannot.

REALISM

Proponents of realism in philosophy include Greek philosopher Aristotle (384-322 BC), Niccolo Machiavelli (1469-1527, philosopher during the Renaissance in Italy), John Locke (1632-1704, English philosopher and physician, considered the father of classical liberalism), and David Hume (1711-1776, Scottish philosopher), and Hans Morgenthau (1904-1980, political realist).

Contemporary philosophical realism is the belief that our reality, or some aspect of it, is independent of our conceptual schemes, linguistic practices, beliefs, and so on. On the other hand, platonic realism is a philosophical term usually used to refer to the idea of realism regarding the existence of universals or abstract objects after the Greek philosopher Plato (c. 427–c. 347 BC), a student of Socrates.

Realists see the world in terms of objects and matter. To some extent, the realist perspective is in contrast to idealism, in that realists believe that our perceptions through our senses provide the context for the human experience. Nature and natural laws are seen and acknowledged through the senses and as long as people conform to these laws, their behavior is rational.

This philosophy can also be described in relation to decision-making. When a person makes a decision, or decides to take an action, there are two extremes available. Aristotle would argue against any one extreme, and instead, strive for the "Golden Mean," which falls in the middle of both polarized extremes.

Fear can just as easily be explained in a realist sense, although the notion of idealism and realism may be considered in opposition to one another. A realist perspective asserts that our perceptions through our senses provide the context for the human experience. Nature and natural laws are seen and acknowledged through our senses and as long as people conform to these laws, a person's behavior is rational.

The very essence of fear is instinctive. A person is born with an innate concept of fear as a means of survival. However, what we fear over time is learned, based on our environment and our experiences. We learn to fear certain things because we have either been actually harmed by something, or we have been taught that something has the potential to harm us. When we act, we typically do so in a way that is rational and in accordance with what we know to be true of the world around us. When others act, they are doing so in a way that is rational and in accordance what they know of the world.

The basic, core realism suggests that our perceptions, through our senses, provide the context for the human experience. Nature and natural laws are seen and acknowledged through the senses and as long as people conform to these laws, their behavior is rational. Now consider the METUS Principle. The very notion of fear serves as the cornerstone for the human experience as it relates to natural law. Our fear is experienced through our senses: what we see, what we touch, what we smell, what we hear, and what we taste. These senses are connected with what it is to be human.

The METUS Principle can be used to help explain the world around us. Some experiences will validate or reinforce our fear. For example, if a child ever touches a hot stove or is burned by fire, he or she realizes there is a good reason to be afraid of things that are hot and things that can burn. If a person is ever attacked by an animal or person, he or she will likely remember sounds, smells, and images, of what was going on during the attack. This memory of experiences and events will be something individuals hold on to, and if they find themselves in a similar scenario, they will likely experience a heightened sense of anxiety and fear. They have recognized that certain environmental conditions and experiences are associated with danger.

In the case of touching fire, or something that is hot, the answer may be as simple as not touching it. With regard to being attacked by man or beast, people can avoid environments and situations that put them in increased risk of injury or harm. If they chose to place themselves in a similar environment, they could also carry protection for defense. In both cases, their fear of injury was validated and as a result, they were faced with the need to recognize, understand, and manage their fear for future similar encounters.

However, not everything in life is a simple and straightforward. There are many experiences in life that are fleeting, and come and go without our giving them much thought. Nonetheless, with every passing minute we learn. Even events that are innocuous carry lessons and have significance.

When Kensington was two years old, Halloween took on new meaning for her. One day, we went over to my mother- and father-in-law's house shortly after they put up their decorations. As soon as we arrived, Kensington immediately panicked and was terrified at the sight of witches, skeletons, and Frankenstein. My older daughter screamed and wanted to go home. She ran to me, jumped into my arms, and held on tight for dear life, while at the same time screaming and crying. Of course, I tried to console her and tell her they were just decorations.

After comforting her for a few moments until she stopped crying, I attempted to have a conversation with her. I explained to her what decorations were, why we put them out for Halloween, and told her that they are considered fun. It was probably way more information than was needed, and certainly more than she would have been able to fully understand, but I thought it was important to talk with her about them.

I then asked Kensington questions about witches, about Frankenstein, and about the skeletons. I asked her what color each was, which one she was most afraid of, why she didn't like them, and other simple, age-appropriate questions. When I asked her, "Why don't you like them?" she replied, "Because they are scary."

After that, I proceeded to ask probing questions, "Why are they scary?" to which she said, "Because I don't like them. They are scary." I continued to ask, "Why are they scary?" Then I explained to her that she didn't need to be afraid of them and that the decorations wouldn't hurt her. I repeatedly told her that they are fun, and after slowly approaching the decorations, I reached out to touch Frankenstein and the skeleton. She immediately had a meltdown and started crying, but I quickly cut her off and said, "Look, Daddy is okay. They are just decorations and they won't hurt us." I touched the decorations and played with them. It wasn't long that she realized they weren't hurting us.

Now, it didn't mean she liked them right away, but it was a step in the right direction. It took weeks, and several more trips to Grandma and Grandpa's before she truly became desensitized to them. Each time we visited, I applied the METUS Principle to help her through her innate fear. I asked her to confirm or recognize what she was afraid of. Then I talked with her to help me understand why she was afraid. Once we knew what she was afraid of, and why she was afraid, we talked about why there was no reason to be afraid and spent time confirming my statements to her.

Her daddy played with the decorations, was laughing, having a good time, and Kensington saw they were not hurting me. She managed her fear and eventually touched one of them. I laughed and had her do it again, this time knocking one out of my hand. Again, she laughed. After one or two more times, she wasn't afraid to touch the once scary monsters. She now had no reason to be afraid, because her experiences with each of the decorations taught her that they were not going to cause her any harm. By the end of Halloween, they were fun for her! Even the candy bowl, with the moving hand and creepy music, was no big deal. This was the METUS Principle at work!

PRAGMATISM

People who are considered pragmatists in the philosophical sense include William James (1842–1910, American philosopher, psychologist, and physician), Charles Sanders Peirce (1839–1914, mathematician and founder of American pragmatism), and George Herbert Mead (1863–1931, American philosopher, sociologist and psychologist).

Pragmatism, unlike idealism and realism, was developed with contemporary, rather than traditional, undertones. The model itself places value in change, process, and relativity. Both idealism and realism emphasize subject matter truths and laws, whereas pragmatism suggests that reality is always changing. Because reality is always changing, there cannot be any universal or absolute truths, nor can there be natural laws that are fixed.

As people attempt to solve a problem, they are participants in change and are able to witness how their environment is constantly changing. Someone who subscribes to pragmatic principles is saying, "What was true yesterday is not necessarily true today."

We are guided by what we know, but understand that we must be willing to accept that things do change. Thus what we know to be true today may not always be true tomorrow. Pragmatists always consider the million-dollar question: "Why?" They then look for ways to view that "why" in terms of who, what, where, when, and how.

Being open to change, pragmatists then look toward the next important question, which is: "What if?" This constant questioning is the basis of scientific reasoning.

John Dewey (1859-1952), American philosopher, psychologist and educational reformer, believed that the pragmatic approach is the ultimate process through which to improve the human condition.

When we look at the behavior of other people, we may perceive them as acting in a manner that is irrational because their behaviors are not consistent with our own understanding of the world. Since we all have different and unique experiences, our perception of our environment and natural laws varies to some degree.

Every interaction we have with others and with our environment shapes our concept of the individual human experience. Throughout each person's life, he or she experiences, understands, and manages his or her fears differently and yet, one fact remains constant: one person's fears are no less real to him than another's are to that individual.

Perhaps one of the simplest philosophical theories for understanding fear is the pragmatic framework. Pragmatism suggests that reality is always changing. Because reality is always changing, there cannot be any universal or absolute truths, nor can there be natural laws that are fixed. What a person fears, and certainly to what extent those fears play in his or her life, are not universal.

Every person is afforded a unique perspective on life based on personal interactions and exchanges with others and with his or her environment. Furthermore, the better a person is at recognizing his or her fears, understanding those fears, and managing them, the better he or she can navigate through life in a way that allows maximization of his or her potential.

Consider life as the ultimate obstacle course with a number of different barriers and hurdles each person must face. An obstacle course is a great analogy, because an obstacle course requires people to recognize the challenges immediately before them, develop an understanding and strategy for overcoming those challenges, and acting upon what they know and the strategy they decided upon, in order to successfully complete the course. In some cases, a person may not have selected the best strategy, and as a result, did not successfully overcome a particular barrier. For some obstacles, participants may take short cuts or side-step particular barriers, accept a penalty, and move on, while when faced with other obstacles, they cannot.

The same holds true in life. Some situations in life require people to address an immediate barrier before they can successfully move on; other times, they are able to side-step the barrier and accept whatever penalty is associated with doing so. Every one of us faces a different obstacle course, with different barriers, each and every day of our lives.

Our environment and the challenges we face shape who we are as individuals, which is why our reality, according to pragmatic philosophy, is always changing. As we learn to navigate through life, we continuously face different barriers and challenges. Many people may find themselves stuck because they have been unwilling or unable to move past a barrier that is preventing them from advancing.

Fear is one of the major obstacles we confront. It can stop us in our tracks, or if we have a strategy in place for recognizing it, understanding it, and then managing that fear, we are able to negotiate the course successfully as we move toward our individual finish lines.

EXISTENTIALISM

Philosophers and writers, such as Søren Kierkegaard (Danish, 1813-1855), Fyodor Dostoyevsky (Russian, 1821-1881), Friedrich Nietzsche (German, 1844-1900), and Jean-Paul Sartre (French, 1905-1980) were proponents of the existentialist philosophy.

The most important consideration for the individual is the fact that he or she is an individual—an independently acting and responsible conscious being ("existence")—rather than what labels, roles, stereotypes, definitions, or other preconceived categories the individual fits ("essence"). This school of thought gives priority to concrete human reality over abstract thinking, and highlights the importance of personal choice and commitment.

Existentialism is the latest and most modern approach to philosophical thinking. Following World War II, there was a shift in Western thinking that began to deemphasize the group and emphasize individualism. It was a push for people to reach self-fulfillment through personal endeavors.

Existentialists are not concerned with group norms, trends, authority, customs, traditions, or any other outside factor(s) that would limit a person's individuality. Existentialism deemphasizes the group and emphasizes the individual. Existentialism is grounded in the desire to push people to reach self-fulfillment through personal endeavors. Each individual makes choices that define who he or she is, which in turn is dependent on the actions he or she takes (or does not take) in life.

Each person's perspective is unique because it is the evolutionary result of unique interactions with other people, experiences, and the individual's environment. No two people on Earth, not even identical twins, experience life in exactly the same fashion. As a result, no two people have exactly the same perspective on life. Existentialism places a greater emphasis on the individual because each person's potential varies in accordance with his or her unique perspectives. Every person has a varying degree of potential because he or she possesses varying degrees of what is actual.

With every interaction, every experience, and every lesson, we are forever changed. The entire notion of "group think," or group equality, deemphasizes unique experiences and inherently limits the potential of every single person within a group. Existentialists are not concerned with group norms, trends, authority, customers, traditions, or any other outside factor(s) that would limit a person's individuality. Instead, they encourage every individual to be the best he or she can be. From a purely common sense approach, existentialism promotes human efficiency, and in doing so, produces a greater overall benefit to the entire group.

I believe that fear is the driving principle in how people navigate through life. If a person's actual fear is great enough, he or she will be motivated to recognize, understand, and manage that fear as a matter of survival. If the actual fear is not as great as the potential fear, he or she will be content with the current state and not motivated to take action to overcome a most immediate barrier.

SUMMARY

As I considered the four major schools of philosophy, the first question I asked myself was: "Can the METUS

Principle be applied to each of them, and if so, how?" This question and its answer were important to me because the answer would reveal whether or not my concept was universally applicable.

Consider the goal of philosophy: to aspire to finding a universal truth and produce propositions that would be acceptable to any rational person, anywhere, at any time. Furthermore, it is not only my contention that the METUS Principle is such a universal truth, but also that it is the origin of the human experience—in other words, the lowest common denominator.

For fear to be considered the lowest common denominator, I would have to be able to explain my concept within the context and framework of the other great philosophical works across time. I believe I was able to do so and as a result I remain confident that the METUS Principle better simplifies human behavior and motivation than does any concept that has preceded it.

Idealism suggests that reality, or reality as we can know it, is fundamentally mental, mentally constructed, or otherwise immaterial. The METUS Principle suggests that the most basic innate characteristic of the human experience is the feeling of fear. A fear, whether produced by the brain or created by the soul, is otherwise immaterial. A person cannot touch fear or hold fear, but it is real and it is experienced by each and every one of us in a personal way. Likewise, each of us can come to recognize, understand, and manage our fear.

When we come to accept fear, we can then learn what it is that we are afraid of. While fear is mentally constructed and internal, what we are afraid of is often external. When we recognize what we are afraid of, and understand why we are afraid of it, we can then change our behavior to manage our fear. By managing our fear, we function better in our environment. The better we function, and the more productive we are, the more we advance to the point of becoming self-actualized.

Realists see the world in terms of objects and matter. Realists believe that the perceptions we receive through our senses provide the context for the human experience: sight, hearing, smell, taste, and touch. Our senses evaluate our experiences, what we perceive happening to us at any given moment. Without our senses, we wouldn't know what to be afraid of. However, we would still possess fear. This is because fear exists in each of us, whether or not we can experience, identify, or communicate what we are afraid of—or not. In other words, what we are afraid of and can identify through our five senses are merely physical manifestations of our fear.

Pragmatism places value in change, process, and relativity. Pragmatism suggests that reality is always changing. The METUS Principle both recognizes and appreciates change. A person's experiences, how he or she perceives and internalizes experiences, and the actions subsequently taken, will all impact that individual's reality. Who a person is, is different than who they were, and different than who they will be in the future, because every experience in a person's life leaves an impression.

An impression, based on even a innocuous or mundane experience, may be ever so slight, even to the point we may not consciously acknowledge its effect, but it is nonetheless there. Every moment in our lives forever changes who are, the choices we make, and how we view the world around us. From a pragmatic perspective, this is why I place such a heavy emphasis on recognizing, understanding, and managing fear. These three processes are empowering and allow a person to actively be a change agent and engage in processes, so that he or she may progress toward becoming a self-actualized version of him or herself.

I place a heavy emphasis on change and processes, recognizing that our actual self and our potential self are necessarily different. We can never actually be and potentially be the same person, because every experience we have changes us in some way. However, I disagree with the pragmatic assertion that there can be no absolute truth. I contest that fear itself is absolute. However, consistent with the pragmatic perspective, I believe that what we are afraid of is not fixed, will change over time, and is dependent on how we perceive and respond to a particular environmental experience.

Existentialism gives priority to concrete human reality over abstract thinking, and highlights the importance of personal choice and commitment. Existentialism was a drive toward reaching self-fulfillment through personal endeavors and asserts that the choices an individual makes defines who he or she is. Who a person is, is dependent on the actions he or she takes (or does not take) in life.

Existentialism speaks to the empowering and deterministic element of the METUS Principle. A person's reality is fixed, based on his or her environment, choices, and actions. What is, is. However, while a person's reality is fixed, his or her potential is not. What individuals can become is not so much a function of who they are, but what they are willing to do in order to achieve that in which they wish to become.

At birth, we are all more or less created the same. No one is born anything, much less a baker, a teacher, a lawyer, or a doctor. What we become is dependent on our individual efforts and the choices we make. If a student wishes to become a doctor, he or she is the only thing standing in the way. The choices the student makes, and his or her effort, will determine whether or not the dream of becoming a doctor is realized. It is not up to anyone else or the Universe; it is up to the individual.

An argument can be made, and often is, that there are always variable factors. Factors such as genetic makeup, cognitive/emotional/social abilities, and external environmental factors that cannot be controlled by an individual. I do not disagree that these variables are important. My counterargument is that not everyone has the same version of *ideal self*. Not everyone wants to be a baker, a teacher, a lawyer, or a doctor. Our ideal self is a product of many of these variable factors and each one of us develops a version of our ideal self taking these variables into consideration. However, just because someone in a particular environment may have a more difficult journey toward achieving one's dream, it does not mean the dream is unattainable. Conversely, just because someone else may have an easier path, it does not guarantee that they will achieve their dream either. We are all unique, and no two people's paths in life are the same.

For this reason, within the METUS Principle, I identify the importance of recognizing, understanding, and managing fear. Fear can be limited and even debilitating; and it can also be motivating and empowering. Fear is a catalyst and will cause a person to act. A person's choice is just that—personal. Choice will ultimately impact the person's reality. The more a person recognizes, understands, and manages fear, the greater the likelihood of reaching self-fulfillment through personal endeavors.

The METUS Principle can, and does, integrate nicely with each of these four major philosophies. Because the METUS Principle is universally applicable, it can be used to further explain each philosophy as it examines and explains conditions related to the human experience.

Perspective	Description
Idealism	The desire to discover absolute or universal truth.
Realism	Our perceptions through our senses provide the context for the human experience.
Pragmatism	Reality is always changing, and therefore, there cannot be any universal or absolute truths, nor fixed natural laws.
Existentialism	Every individual is an independently acting and responsible conscious being.

NOTES

CHAPTER THREE

MEDICAL VALIDATION FOR THE METUS PRINCIPLE

Christine Wodke's Story:
Author and Athlete

When you think of elite athletes or runners. Chris Wodke may not be the first name that comes to mind. She is a three-time qualifier for the Boston Marathon and placed second overall in her division in 2012. As a triathlete, completing nationally in 2013 at the National Sprint Championship in Austin, Texas, Wodke finished in first place in 2012 and second place in 2013. She also took home first place as a triathlete in the Midwest Regionals in 2013. Her ultimate dream, and goal, would be to represent the United States of America in the Paralympic Games in 2016. Yet, despite Chris's remarkable achievements, very few sports fans are familiar with her name.

The reason you may not have heard of Chris is because she is, in fact, a para-athlete. In 2010, at the age of 55, Chris Wodke was diagnosed with a neuromuscular disease called Charcot-Marie-Tooth, or CMT for short. CMT is a disease of the nerves that control muscles, causing loss of normal function and/or sensation in the lower legs and feet, as well as arms and hands. Additional symptoms of CMT may include fatigue, sleep apnea, loss of sensation, difficulty with balance and walking, breathing difficulties, and poor tolerance for cold temperatures. Patients with CMT can have trouble doing even simple everyday tasks involving manual dexterity, such as writing, opening jars, and even manipulating buttons and zippers.

In addition to being an accomplished athlete. Chris is the Founder and Manager of Team CMT. Team CMT was created to raise awareness for Charcot-Marie-Tooth and also to raise money to support research and treatment. Since its creation in 2011, Team CMT has gained over 120 members in the United States, as well as Canada. Wodke has written a book called, *Running for My Life – Winning for CMT*. And if all of these accolades weren't enough, Chris has accomplished these tasks in addition to working her full -time job as an engineer for Wisconsin Energies.

When I met with Chris in 2014, I was excited to talk with her. Many people diagnosed with a medical condition, particularly one like CMT, would tend to see the ailment as enough of a reason to take it easy. Yet, Chris was compelled to do just the opposite. Rather than use CMT as an excuse to take it easy, at 55 years of age, Chris used her diagnoses as motivation.

Prior to meeting with Chris, I spent some time reading articles online, reviewing her website, and reading her blog. As I combed through documents, I came across a statement she offered on her Team CMT website. The paragraph was as followed:

When I was in graduate school for engineering, I had to take a thermodynamics class that required mathematically solving the laws of the physical science and its effect on material bodies. We were presented with pages and pages of equations, which had to be dissected to prove the theories of our homework. Also part of the class requirement was to meet with the professor each week to review assignments. One day he said to me, "Christine, you get so close to solving the problem, but then you quit."

That single sentence offered to her by her professor during a weekly meeting, has always stuck with her. Since that time, when faced with obstacles or challenges in life, she has been determined not to give up too soon. When things get tough, and she feels like quitting, she wonders to herself how close she is to achieving her goal – and it is that drive that pushes her to keep going.

During our meeting, I asked her to expand on this lesson offered to her, and what it means exactly to her today as she faces new types of challenges, as well as new goals. Of course, when of the first questions I asked her was, "Why marathons and triathlons? Given symptoms like numbness in one's extremities, fatigue, and breathing difficulties, why would you choose these particular sports or events?" Confidently, she looked at me and said that is was because of these demands, in large part, that she chose them. She wants to stay active, and keep her muscles as strong as she can for as long as she can.

In her personal life, she considers herself a bit of a risk-taker – and someone who refuses to hold back. Choosing to confront her condition head on, with rigorous activities such as distance running and triathlons, was her was of taking control of her situation. Rather than let CMT establish her limits, she was determined to test them, and over time with proper training and effort, raise them.

Given my research and interests, I asked her whether or not fear served as a motivating influence in her life. In one word, she responded, "Absolutely." She continued, "I feel that I manage my fear by being prepared and by working hard." Taking a second to pause, she recalled a favorite quote of hers, and one she thinks about before starting a race. She attributes it to Alberto Salazar and said, "At the starting line, we are all cowards."

Thinking about that quote helps her put her own fear into perspective. Prior to beginning any race, our minds race and we wonder what will be. It is at that moment, standing among the masses, in which we have no control. However, when the gun goes off and the race begins, all participants need to decide how badly they want it, how badly they want to win – or even in some cases, how badly they want to finish.

I asked her in what other ways has she experienced fear related to her diagnoses or training. As far as the diagnoses, she told me that she was actually relieved when she was told she had CMT.

"Relieved?" I asked.

"I had known that something was not right, physically, for years. I experienced fatigue, as well as numbness and tingling, and the CMT diagnoses would explain these things. So yes, I was actually relieved."

From a training standpoint, she recalled a moment she referred to as her "ah hah!" moment. During a coaching session, she remembered a time that she had been taught to replace fear with a positive or productive thought. In baseball, for example—thinking or saying the words, "Bounce and hit", can replace the thought, "I hope I don't miss," her coach had said to her. Using this lesson, she transferred this thought process into her own life, particularly when swimming and while training for triathlons. Instead of thinking, "I could drown," she instead began to think to herself, "Turn and breathe." Her coach insisted that, "The mind can only focus and concentrate on one thought at a time...so you might as well make it a positive and productive one!" she said.

Of course, I would be remiss if I did not ask her about her experiences at the Boston Marathon. Her first race, in 2012, was especially nerve-racking for her. This was a big stage. Because the Boston Marathon is a big deal, a lot of people were now noticing her. She was giving interviews, her face was on television, and her story in magazines, and with the attention, a scary thought crept into her mind, "What if I don't finish?" She was afraid of the very thought that, if she didn't finish, she would let people down. It wasn't that she wasn't in good shape, it wasn't that she wouldn't give it her all, and to even get in the Boston Marathon she had to prove herself in other marathons. But despite all of the great things Chris had going for her, she realized that anything could happen.

At Boston, the temperature reached 90+ degrees. She could get a cramp, heat fatigue, or other serious injury that would be beyond her control. Four hundred people or more each year start the race and never finish. As she stood at the starting line, about to run the biggest race of her life up to that point, she realized that public failure is very scary. But despite her fear, despite all of the things that could go wrong, despite the possibility of public failure, Chris was determined to give it her best – her real, honest, genuine, best. Whatever would happen at that point would be beyond her control. Ultimately, Chris would not only finish, but take 2nd place in the mobility-impaired division. Her first time running Boston was a success.

In 2013, Chris returned to Boston after coming off a championship in the Midwest Regional Female Paratriathlon in Omaha, Nebraska. Although back on the big stage,

Chris was not as worried this time around. After finishing second the previous year, and training hard since that time, she felt that her preparation and hard work over the past year would serve her well.

What she was not prepared for—and in fact no one was—was the act of terrorism and violence that would occur near the finish line at 2:49 pm EDT. The bombs exploded 12 seconds apart, 210 yards away, killing three innocent people and injuring over 260 others.

Wodke was at mile 23 when the bombs went off. She ran with a guide and shortly after the explosion, her guide's phone lit up with people asking if she was okay. Chris simply thought it was an accident of some sort – a transformer or manhole accident—and was not as worked up about it early on as others were. However, gradually more and more information would be released, and eventually, she and others would learn the explosions were no accident.

I asked Chris to describe to me the events, and her perspective, after she learned what had in fact happened. Following the bombing, many of her friends and other racers were afraid to go out. Chris wasn't. She was eager to go out. She wanted to talk with people and hear their thoughts. She wasn't afraid to ask, "Where were you when the bombs went off"…or answer that question when it was asked of her. She felt that it was important to talk about the incident – to share and hear from others, racers and members of the public. As far as any long-term effects from her experience, Chris said the Boston Bombing has changed her perspective some. The fact is, "Experiences change reality," she said.

She recalled a race where she had volunteered to work down on Milwaukee's lakefront. She was at the finish line October after the bombings, and she remembers thinking, "It could happen here. Really, it could happen anywhere."

As we neared the end of our conversation, I asked Chris, "Do you believe it is possible to grow as a person, achieve success, or be happy in life, without learning how to manage fear?"

She replied, "No, I doubt it. Fear is a lock that holds us back and keeps us from realizing our full potential. Managing fear is the key that unlocks the potential in us." She thought about her own experiences, and once again thought back to comments made to her by her graduate school professor.

"You need to keep you goal in mind. You cannot allow you fear to take over. Being mentally strong is as important, if not more important, than being physically strong. Where your mind goes, your body will follow. It starts here," she said, pointing to her head, "and here," pointing to her heart. "You have to always keep climbing. Don't be afraid to fall – and if you do fall, get right back up and keep climbing again."

She continued, "I believe athletes are better pre-pared to cope with fear and face adversity because sport trains us to. Athletes constantly have to continue to work, get better, and even deal with losses. Any of the medals and awards that are earned are tangible symbols that validate a person's effort, and they feel good. They feel good because of what they represent—all of your hard work."

Although there is no cure for CMT, that hasn't stopped Chris for accomplishing her goals and achieving new heights. Because Chris has learned to recognize, un-derstand, and manage her fear, she has been able to overcome obstacles in her life that she could have just as easily used to create excuses. I wish Chris the best of luck as she continues to unlock her own potential, prepare for future races – and hopefully receive the opportunity to realize her dream of competing in the Paralympic games in Rio in 2016.

* * * * *

Fear stifles our thinking and our actions.
It creates indecisiveness that results in stagnation.
I have known talented people who procrastinate
indefinitely rather than risk failure.
Lost opportunities cause the erosion of confidence
and the downward spiral begins.
—Charles Stanley

Paul Tough has written an outstanding book, *How Children Succeed: Grit, Curiosity, and the Hidden Power of Character,* which compiles significant medical research and a number of examples that highlight the impacts that [fear and] stress have on people. His research shows that although brain shaping and behavioral patterns occur most noticeably in younger years, brain development affects how people behave, as well as their decision-making processes, throughout their lives.

Research supporting biological effects related to changes in decision-making behaviors come from two notable, but rather obscure, areas of science. The first is neuroendocrinology, which is the study of the interaction between the nervous system and the endocrine system. Neuroendocrinologists research how hormones interact with the brain. The nervous and endocrine systems often act together in a process called neuroendocrine integration, to regulate the physiological [chemical] processes of the human body.

The second discipline that studies how the brain and body interact is physiology. Specifically, physiologists study function in living systems (biology). Within physiology is an even more specific focus known as stress physiology. Stress physiology is the study of how stress affects the body.

While areas like psychology and psychiatry attempt to explain the relationship between environments and human behavior, neuroendocrinology and stress physiology seek to explain what happens to the brain and body when a person encounters a particular environmental stimuli.

The first study noted by Tough was attributed to Burke Harris and is known as the "Adverse Childhood Experiences" (ACE) study. Burke attempted to scientifically explain the effects of fear, and the lurking and lasting impacts that remain with people in the depths of human biology—at least until they learn how to recognize, understand, and manage, fear's effects. Those who study ACE contend that stress effects can be seen at a molecular level, and become part of a person's biological makeup. Such researchers generally come from within the medical field and study either neuroendocrinology, stress physiology, or both.

According to ACE research, our bodies regulate stress using a system called the hypothalamus-pituitary-adrenal, or HPA, axis. HPA describes the way that chemical signals navigate through our brain and our body during times that are stressful and intense. When we come across a situation that evokes a stress [fear] response, usually at the onset of a proposed threat or danger, this experience triggers activity in our hypothalamus. The hypothalamus is the region of our brain that regulates unconscious biological processes, such as body temperature, hunger, and thirst. Activity in our hypothalamus sets off a chain reaction, starting with a signal that it sends to receptors in our pituitary glands. The pituitary glands send out a hormone to stimulate our adrenal glands and finally our adrenal glands trigger the production of our actual stress hormones, called glucocorticoids.

Glucocorticoids are responsible for activating an array of defense responses which include, but are not limited to, an increased heart rate, clammy skin, and dry mouth. There are also additional effects of the HPA axis that are less immediately apparent, even during actual periods of stress. These other reactions may include the activation of neurotransmitters, rise in glucose levels, and increased blood flow sent to muscles by our cardiovascular system. The increased blood flow carries with it inflammatory proteins, which rush through the bloodstream.

This entire process is explained within the context of psychology as the "fight, freeze, or flight" response. Increased blood flow, along with inflammatory proteins, which occur in response to a perceived harmful event, are hardwired and are a biological survival instinct.

In the modern era, by and large, most people do not face the same types of threats that our primitive survival instincts served. In civil society, we do not run the risk of encountering large predators as our ancestors did when they were hunters and gatherers. Today, each person experiences different sources of stress in his or her own environment.

Because modern humans find themselves worrying less about predators, modern sources of stress tend to be issues related to finances, relationships, and time management. However, a major problem we face is that we end up activating the same hormones that previously served the biological purpose primarily related to self-preservation. This system was meant to be a short-term, acute response for emergencies.

Once our primitive ancestors were no longer in danger, their brains stopped producing stress hormones. What researchers are learning is that while our societal stresses produce the same biological responses as an acute emergency, once activated, we have a difficult time turning them off. When activated, our stress responses may stay on for weeks, if not months. This extended activation of our stress system is not only unnecessary, but also highly destructive to our biological system.

Overloading the HPA axis, especially early in life during early physical and cognitive development stages, can produce serious and potentially damaging, negative effects. Because of the chemical reactions, overactive and sustained activity by the HPA axis can adversely affect physical, psychological, and neurological development, particularly in children.

If you have read this chapter carefully so far, you will notice that it isn't actually fear, or stress itself, that damages the body. It is the body's [chemical] reaction to fear and stress that it harmful.

Now consider the METUS Principle. Starting with Maslow's hierarchy, we know we all have needs, some of which are more basic than others. The more needs we have met, and the extent to which they are met, determine our level of fear and the biological effects we experience.

If our needs are not sufficiently met, or have not been met for an extended period of time, our level of fear increases. As our level of fear increases, our bodies respond accordingly. Very quickly, we can find ourselves in a tailspin and living a life in which our fear manages us, instead of us managing our fear.

Because the biological consequences can be so damaging, it is important to develop coping mechanisms to preempt this reaction and reduce the amount of activity triggered in our HPA axis. To do this, we have to work on **recognizing** what we are afraid or fearful of, **understanding** why it is we are afraid; and start to develop actionable plans that will help us take control of and **manage** those fears. We have to consciously and proactively take action that is directed at managing our level of fear and stress so that we can reduce the amount of activity taking place in our HPA axis.

Consider the question of whether actions precede feelings or feelings precede actions. When a person is sad, it has been scientifically proven that if another can induce that person to smile, it will trigger responses in the brain that release the same chemicals as those released when we are happy. While individuals might not have experienced anything to make them happy, forcing a smile will nonetheless produce a similar biological effect—albeit in a much smaller dose.

Managing fear does NOT mean suppressing it. Managing fear is a personal choice to take action to address issues that concern for a person—the key word here being **action**. Since fear is a catalyst and a motivating force for people to act, it is important to learn ways address fear through actions that are positive and help achieve more positive outcomes. This in effect will reduce our level of stress. Managing fear positively will not only produce more desirable psychological effects, but also more desirable biochemical results as well.

Bruce McEwen is a neuroendocrinologist at Rockefeller University, and he has proposed a theory of managing stress he calls "allostasis." According to McEwen, allostasis is a process that causes wear and tear on the body. When the body remains in a constant state of stress, or the body's stress management system is overworked, eventually the body encounters problems as a result of the strain. He calls these problems "allostatic load," and according to McEwen, the effects of constant stress [fear] can be seen physically throughout a person's body. The primitive and survival effects can be seen when acute stress raises blood pressure, and provides increased blood flow to muscles and organs, in an effort to prepare for a potentially dangerous situation.

As mentioned above, this is often referred to as a "fight or flight" response. However, frequent and sustained elevated blood pressure leads to atherosclerotic plaque. This additional plaque causes heart attacks.

In addition to McEwen's work, stress physiologists have found biological evidence that stress likely alters parts of the brain, which in turn results in changes in how a person processes information. The prefrontal cortex is the part of the brain most affected by early stress, which is critical in self-regulatory activities of all kinds, both emotional and cognitive. Studies have shown that children who grow up in stressful environments are more likely to have problems concentrating, sitting still, and have a harder time recovering from disappointing experiences. Children who grow up in stressful environments also demonstrate a greater tendency to follow directions. (Sources for the studies are provided in the Resources section of this book.)

This research is not at all surprising to me. Again, think about the METUS Principle. At the base of Maslow's pyramid, we have physiological needs, then safety needs, and then needs for love and belonging. It is very unlikely that a child—or for that matter, an adult—in a stressful environment, is able to have these three important levels of need satisfied. Whether it is a lack of food or clean water, or living in an unsafe environment, or growing up in a situation void of love and support, young children most often do not have the mental maturity to recognize how fearful they are, at least not in the sense that they are consciously aware. They are unable to make sense of their environments or understand their fear; and as a result, they are unable to manage their fears.

Children in fear live moment to moment, and develop behaviors and mental thought processes that heavily emphasize causal thinking tendencies—in other words, "What do I actually need to do?" Because they are overwhelmed, they are not able to spend much effort developing corollary thinking skills or able to think ahead to alternative futures based on a series of choices.

When a child fails to develop corollary thinking skills, the brain wires itself along accustomed pathways. As a result, over time, such children's brains become wired in a way that struggles to control impulses, is distracted by negative feelings, and retains fear. Although circumstances and environments may change, the fear stays with them and is part of their biological make-up.

Depending on the type of experiences that reinforced a child's fear and the period of time a child experienced fear, it may be very difficult and take a significant amount of time to help the child reduce that fear. To reduce the fear, such children will have to eventually recognize, understand, and manage their fear, which requires a very introspective process. It also requires experiences that are positive and directed at meeting their needs to begin progressing upward through Maslow's hierarchy.

Once more basic needs are met, a person will begin to think beyond the "here and now" and start to develop pathways that support corollary or long-term thought processes.

As far as brain development is concerned, some effects of stress in the prefrontal cortex can be described as emotional or psychological, as well as causing anxiety and depression.

Lawrence Steinburg, a psychologist at Temple University, has recognized two separate neurological systems that develop in childhood and early adulthood and together have a profound effect on the decision-making patterns and habits of adolescents. It is in early childhood that our brains and bodies are most sensitive to the effects of stress and trauma, but it is in adolescence that the damage stress inflicts can lead to the most serious and long-lasting problems.

According to Steinburg, the first neurological system is known as the "incentive processing system." This system makes a person more sensation-seeking, emotionally reactive, and more attentive to social information. The second is called the "cognitive control system." This second system allows a person to regulate the urges of the incentive system.

From the perspective of the METUS Principle, the incentive processing system would be the system that supports a causal thought process: "If I do [this], the outcome will be [that]." This is simple cause-and-effect thinking and does not require much higher level cognition.

The cognitive control system, on the other hand, is more refined. It takes into account a person's immediate impulse to do something, and regulates behaviors based on assessing a number of variables, goals, and a range of possible outcomes. The cognitive control system allows a person to think in a corollary fashion: "If I do [this..or that], [these] are the possible outcomes associated with each possible choice I could make. "

Steinburg says that the incentive processing system reaches its full power in early adolescence and the cognitive control system doesn't finish maturing until a person reaches the twenties. However, just because the two systems don't mature until certain phases in life, this does not mean they entirely lack any ability to process information earlier in life. A young child may have some capabilities of each and the extent to which a child will process information will vary.

Since 2010, researchers at Northwestern University gave psychiatric evaluations to more than a thousand detainees at the Cook County Juvenile Detention Center in Chicago. Researchers found that:

- 84 percent of detainees had experienced two or more serious childhood traumas (the majority had experienced 6 or more)
- 75 percent of detainees witnessed someone being killed or seriously injured
- More than 40 percent of female detainees had been sexually abused as children
- More than 50 percent of boys reported that at least once, they had been in situations so perilous they thought they, or people close to them, were about to die or become badly wounded.

According to the study, as a result of these major traumas, two-thirds of the males had one or more diagnosable psychiatric disorders. Academically, they were severely behind. Detainees in the study had average scores on standardized vocabulary tests at the fifth percentile, meaning they were below 95 percent of their peers nationwide.

From the perspective of the METUS Principle, these findings are not surprising. Detainees grew up in an environment that required them to operate using a primitive mindset that relied more heavily on fight or flight. They were learning and training their brains to survive, and in doing so, severely limited their ability to develop higher–level cognitive thinking skills. They were forced to focus on causal decision-making processes, earlier described as the incentive processing system.

Because they experienced such intense fear, and carried that fear with them, they did not learn to think about or consider their futures. Future thinking would have allowed them to develop corollary thinking skills, earlier described as the cognitive control system. As a result, detainees developed aggressive, maladaptive, primitive, behaviors that were advantageous for survival, but socially unacceptable in civil society.

The last study I would like to highlight comes from Michael Meaney, a neuroscientist at McGill University. Meaney is well known for his research with rats. Rats are a popular choice, as far as test subjects go, because the rat brain is very similar to the architecture of the human brain. Meaney's work with his rats examined stress triggers and stress responses, by both younger rats (pups) and their mothers (dams). Researchers discovered that when they held a rat pup, it produced anxiety and a flood of stress hormones in the pup. The dam's licking and grooming following handling produced a counter-effect, reducing the anxiety and surge of stress hormones that had recently been produced.

Interestingly, researchers discovered that the actions of the dam not only produced an immediate effect, but also long-term effects on how rats behaved and their decision-making tendencies. Pups that were held, but comforted immediately by the dam, demonstrated bolder and less anxious tendencies later in life. Pups that were not immediately comforted by the dam demonstrated less confident, more nervous, tendencies.

Multiple tests were conducted to test the behaviors of the rats and each time rats that were comforted and experienced less stress early in life became more confident and less anxious later in life. The rats that were not comforted and experienced more stress early in life became less confident and more anxious.

The study is fascinating because it confirms that brains and behavior patterns develop on the basis of exposure to fear. This means the exact same environmental factors later in life will produce two different, but still predicable, behavioral reactions based on the level and exposure to fear experienced earlier in life and whether or not anything was done to help pups mitigate or manage their fear.

Meaney went even further and was able to discover which part of the pup's genome was "switched on" by licking and grooming. It turned out to be the precise segment that controlled the way the rat's hippocampus would process stress hormones in adulthood. In short, stress raised cortisol production; elevated and sustained increases in cortisol production produce changes in brain development; changes in brain development impact decision-making behaviors; and decision-making behaviors determine how a person progresses along Maslow's hierarchy.

Meaney's study once again validates the METUS Principle. Specifically, his study shows that history and experiences have a continuous effect on development and that fear serves as a catalyst that drives our behavior. We are motivated and wired to do certain [things] based on our experiences in life.

The more stress we have, especially early in life, the more primitively we think and act. The less fear we have, the better we develop, and are able to develop, our higher-level thought processes. In the METUS Principle, these two thought processes are known as **causal** and **corollary** thought processes.

As discussed earlier, at the top of Maslow's hierarchy is self-actualization. Experiencing self-actualization, and becoming self-actualized, is a continuum or progression. It takes time and requires us to progress from the person we are, to the person we want to become—our own personal version of our ideal self. If individuals only develop causal thinking skills, they will be unable to look into the future and envision their ideal self. If they cannot envision their ideal self, they will not be able to develop the corollary thinking skills designed to help them progress from the person they are to the person they want to become.

SUMMARY

Fear in our lives limits our progress and prevents us from becoming self-actualized.

I contend that we can reverse the effects of early and even current sources of fear in our lives. In doing so, we can mitigate the negative effects of fear and stress, and train our brains to develop healthier and more productive decision-making processes.

To mitigate the effects of fear, people must first recognize what they are afraid of. Their fears can stem from their past or exist in the present. More likely than not, it will be a combination of both. Whatever the source of fear, a person must first take an introspective look and be able to positively recognize the source of that fear.

Once individuals recognize the fear or source of the fear, they must then be able to understand it. Understanding fear is often like pulling off a band-aid. It may hurt, and it may uncover old and possibly even painful wounds, but in order to heal, it is important for people to understand their fears.

The final step is taking the fear they have recognized, and have learned to understand, and start to develop strategies for managing it. Managing fear does NOT mean suppressing it; rather, managing fear means owning one's fear.

We have to be willing to accept it and say, "I have been hurt, and I have been afraid, but I will persevere." At that point, individuals are able to identify who they are by virtue of where they came from, and start to consider the future and who they want to become.

NOTES

CHAPTER FOUR

EDUCATION AND FEAR

Dr. Sharon Johnson's Story:
School Superintendent

How did Dr. Sharon Johnson-Shirley become a school superintendent? The short answer is perseverance and hard work. The better question is, how did she become superintendent of the Lake Ridge School District in Gary, Indiana?

The idea of becoming a district leader had not been on her radar screen when it was proposed to her by her predecessor, Dr. Robert Mickey Beach, in the 2002-2003 school year. Her career path was a journey that would take her up through the ranks, assuming more responsibility over time, while at the same time demonstrating her capacity and drive. For fourteen years, she had been a classroom teacher and had obtained an administration degree while working for another school district. For whatever reason—most likely because of district politics—she was unable to get promoted to principal. However, with encouragement from her husband, she began looking for another school district that could utilize her dedication and skills in a leadership role.

The first step on Dr. Johnson-Shirley's path was Dr. Beach's hiring her as principal in the Lake Ridge School District in Gary, Indiana. In short order, she was able to prove her talents and skills as a strong leader, and as a result, Dr. Beach promoted her to Curriculum Director in the Central Office—and later to Assistant Superintendent—all within a five-year time span. Dr. Beach, a constant mentor, also communicated to Sharon that it was his desire to see her become superintendent of Lake Ridge Schools upon his departure.

With Dr. Shirley-Johnson's best interests in mind, Dr. Beach also insisted that she obtain her doctorate, and even brought the application for her to apply to Loyola University in Chicago. He wrote her recommendation letter and she was accepted into the program, which offered a global perspective and gave her the opportunity to study in Rome, Italy, well beyond the academic walls of Indiana and Purdue universities. Dr. Johnson-Shirley received her doctorate on a Sunday and was promoted to superintendent of the Lake Ridge Schools the following Monday.

The disadvantage of being promoted from within is that one does not get a honeymoon period. The expectations are that you know everything you need to know about how to do the job from the moment your nameplate is placed above the door of your new office. Though she thought she was familiar with the inner workings of the district due to her previous position as assistant superintendent, she quickly realized she really didn't have a clue. However, applying one of the lessons learned during her doctoral program, once a position was obtained, she established a baseline on the finances of the district accomplished by means of a district financial audit.

In her first year of becoming superintendent, Dr. Johnson-Shirley discovered that the district had a two-million-dollar deficit. Her immediate task was to create a plan of action as to how the district was going to cut spending and reduce staff. This set off a whirlwind of issues, such as lack of trust by staff and community, not being popular with the staff, and attempts to convince the school board that for the survival of the district, these drastic recommendations must be implemented.

One other major factor was that the district's only high school lacked continuity in hiring principals; over a seven-year span, seven principals had been brought in, only to leave. To add insult to this reality, the Indiana Department of Education under Dr. Tony Bennett, State Superintendent, labeled that high school a "failing school." If improvements were not made, within a year, the state would take over.

This was a difficult time for the district, but also for Dr. Johnson-Shirley as a new superintendent. As a first year superintendent, in a district that had major problems with their finances, and with the risk of being taken over by the state due to failing marks, to say that there were some fearful moments would be putting it mildly.

Despite the obstacles and the many challenges that stood in her way, Dr. Johnson-Shirley understood that attitude was half the battle. Early on in this process, she recognized many of the problems that needed to be addressed, and understood the implications of each for her students, her staff, her district, and her community. All the aforementioned problems were real and she understood that as superintendent, she had to fix what was going wrong in the district – it was up to her to manage the crisis.

A positive thinker by nature, Dr. Johnson-Shirley knew that there were solutions to the district's challenges, and that she had the fortitude to find these and make things happen. Although the problems were many, and some quite complex, each had a solution.

In initial meetings, she invited all of the district stakeholders—teachers, administrators, board members, students, and community members—to be part of the process. She made every effort to keep them informed about the progress along the way, as good leaders tend to do. Also, along with the school board attorney, she requested a meeting with Dr. Tony Bennett to discuss and identify all roles in improving the district. Throughout the process, she was committed to recognizing problems and understanding how they impacted her and her district, so she could make decisions that would help her to manage each critical problem until it was solved.

Dr. Johnson-Shirley's rule number one is that you have to be proactive in finding solutions. There are always going to be problems...and with every problem, there is a corresponding solution. If you do not like your current situation, or your current situation is adversely impacting your ability to move forward and accomplish other goals, then it needs to be addressed.

Leaders, by virtue of their position, are in situations in which they must prioritize issues, make decisions, and find solutions to issues. The issues she faced within her district were very serious and consumed a majority of her energy and time for about two years, but despite the difficulties, she was managing problems, as well as her fear, and she was getting results. Progress was being made.

Throughout the process, she recognized that she did not know everything. Rather than risk making poor decisions in areas she felt she did not fully grasp, she solicited the support and assistance of the State Superintendent in her plan of action. She believed that it was far better to collaborate with someone rather than making excuses as to why something was not working or a problem was not being resolved.

Through strategic planning and thoughtful processing, Dr. Johnson-Shirley successfully led the turn-around-team to a victory of academic success, resulting in the high school being taken off academic probation and increasing the graduation rate from the low seventies to ninety-three percent. The success has been maintained to date.

With support from her leadership team, Dr. Johnson-Shirley has been able to transform the school district into one that was recognized as "An Island of Academic Excellence" by Martha J. Kanter, Under-Secretary, U.S. Department of Education. In addition, Dr. Johnson-Shirley has been recognized by the Board of Education of the Lake Ridge Schools for her unwavering commitment to excellence, and has received numerous awards and certification throughout her career in education.

It is evident that Dr. Johnson-Shirley does not allow fear to stand in her way, or limit her ability to help those around her. She has developed the capacity to recognize, understand, and manage fear in order to improve her district, her community, and the lives of those around her.

* * * * *

Our chief want is someone who will inspire us to be
what we know we could be.
—Ralph Waldo Emerson

One of the most common questions we ask young children is, "So, what do you want to be when you grow up?" We do this to get children thinking about their future. Early on, answers are fairly common and gender related. Little boys typically respond to this question saying they want to be professional athletes, on television or in movies, race car drivers, doctors, president, and many of them want to be their favorite super hero. Little girls typically respond to this question saying they want to be television or movie stars, a veterinarians or zoo keepers, doctors, models, moms, or princesses.

These professions appeal to young children because they represent an idealistic lifestyle. If you pay close attention to a child's response and break it down, it reveals a lot about the natural traits of the child. These traits, when young, are in their early stages of development. Overtime, they will evolve and help shape the person the child will ultimately become at adulthood. The following is an overview of what a child is really telling you.

When children tell you they want to be professional athletes, they may be telling you they want to be seen as strong. Even at a young age, children can pick up on characteristics. They identify athletes as strong people who are gifted at using their body. When children see athletes in the media, people are usually cheering for them. This cheering and admiration further confirms the children's beliefs that these people are special.

When children tell you they want to be actors or actresses, they may be telling you they believe they are creative. There is a side to them that appreciates the arts and would like to perform, they want to be noticed, and seen as attractive. When children watch these people on television or in the movies, they pay close attention to how they carry themselves and consequently, how others are responding to what they do.

When children tell you they want to be doctors or nurses, they may be telling you they have a passion for helping others. When children are young and they are sick or hurt, or when someone they know is sick or hurt, they see a doctor or nurse. Growing up, we all look at doctors as special people with the gift to help others. There is a selfless, giving side to these children who want to make a difference to people in need.

When children tell you they want to be President, or a recognized leader of some sort, they are telling you they are interested in power. There is a side to these children, and a feeling they have, that they were meant to lead others. This is an inner strength that is centered more around intellectual ability than physical.

When children tell you that they want to be parents, they may be telling you they admire what their parents have done or do for them. A child who expresses a desire to become a parent may be expressing a value for love and closeness of family. When children tell you they want to be parents when they grow up, they may be telling you they want to care for others and are concerned more with relationships than external "things." These children find happiness from time spent with others.

When children tell you that they want to be super-heroes, they may be telling you that they want to be important. They want to stand out and want people to take notice. Such children indicate that they want to be superheroes have a belief they have the ability to conquer the world.

It is amazing to listening to children because early on, there is no telling what they will be. It is also amazing to think that the path they take throughout life will have a tremendous impact where they end up.

Children who have dreams follow Freud's principle of the superego, Bronfrenbrenner's principle of the macro-system, Nietzsche's version of the Overman, and John Dewey's concept of self-realization. Young children can "be" anything they want to be in life because they have not yet let fear or other environmental factors, limit their sense of potential.

* * * * *

When we are young, it is very hard conceptualize that daily actions we make each day will have a tremendous impact on the person we become. We simply lack the ability to correlate current actions and future outcomes. For example, if a child is very hard working, goal focused, organized, and determined, those traits will likely transcend a single activity. Adult role models in a child's life play a role in this as well. This is a quintessential example of how nature and nurture impact behavior.

If children are hard working, when it comes to their studies and school, they will likely need little encouragement to stay on top of their work. However, adults can strengthen this characteristic by showing interest and admiration for the child's hard work. On the flip side, if children tend to neglect their studies or is easily side tracked, this too is likely to transcend a single activity.

To allow a child to simply put the work, off or even worse, care little if it is not done at all, is detrimental. To do so enforces a child's poor work habits. Either way, these behaviors early on will pave the way for how a child goes through life.

We need to encourage children, as well as adults, to work toward their dreams, and not to give up on themselves because it seems easier to rely on others.

* * * * *

For countless students each year, school can be a major source of fear. Some students exhibit social anxiety and test-taking anxiety, others may be targeted by bullies, and a significant number of students are faced with learning challenges that qualify as diagnosable disabilities. To say school can be a major source of fear in a child's life is an understatement.

In addition to students' fears, many teachers must face their own fears each day when they walk in their classrooms. Some teachers worry about job security, some worry about job performance, and countless others worry about whether or not they are doing the best job they can for each and every one of their students.

Within this section, I chose to limit my observations and discussion around three key areas: 1) a student's home environment and his or her community, 2) classroom management, and 3) how psychology and philosophy relate to instruction. I have chosen to use examples and intertwine existing theory to illustrate my points.

NATURE VERSUS NURTURE

Historically, there has been great debate focused on whether intelligence is a product of heredity or an individual's environment. The concept of "Nature versus Nurture" was coined in 1869 by Francis Galton. Since that time, professionals in the fields of psychology, education, and educational psychology provided additional insights and perspectives to the discussion.

Those who argue that *nature* plays a dominant role in a person's development believe that a person's DNA, genetics, or heredity largely determine who that person is and the extent of that person's abilities. Proponents of *nurture* playing a dominant role argue that who a person is, and what he or she becomes, is most heavily influenced by the person's environment. While most developmental psychologists today concur that nature and nurture combine to influence development, I have an alternative perspective regarding how nature and nurture relate to one another.

Because learning does not occur in a vacuum, it is incumbent upon each person to learn from his or her environment. One of the first significant research investigations that studied how environmental factors influence education is known as the Coleman Report, which was conducted in the late 1960s. A related study, known as the Jencks Report, was published in the early 1970s. Each study played a considerable role in the field of education because they established that the environment to which a child is exposed is the single greatest factor in determining the child's success or failure.

The Coleman report used a population of n=625,000 students, included students from 4,000 schools, was 1,300 pages long, and comprised 548 pages of statistical data. Perhaps the most troubling finding to come from the report is that teachers and schools have a minimal effect on student achievement. Instead, it was found that a student's home environment significantly outweighed the impacts of teachers in a formal school setting.

Children learn behavior, which carries over into formal schooling. For example, if a student is told by his or her parents that they do not have an education, that school wasn't important to them, and that they have done "ok" for themselves, that message clearly resonates with children. Attending school and learning take effort, and if students are convinced that school is not worth their time or effort, they will not put in the time or work necessary to become successful.

Conversely, for students who grow up in homes that promote school, encourage learning, and teach behaviors that support academic success, those behaviors and values will also carry over into the formal school setting. Such students are more likely to receive positive support at home and have parents who expect their children to put in the time and effort necessary to be successful, which is also learning by example.

Learning is not so much knowing the answer to everything, but understanding how to use resources in order to find answers to questions. Resources are elements and extensions of our environment. Money and time are resources that are finite and most often beyond a child's or student's control (home). However, there are considerable public resources to support education (library), the Internet, and subject matter experts, can all be provided or supported by a school.

The argument in favor of nurture over nature is also supported by Jean Piaget's stages of development. Piaget (1896–1980) was a Swiss developmental psychologist and philosopher known for his theory of cognitive development. Piaget placed great importance on the education of children. Piaget declared in 1934 that "only education is capable of saving our societies from possible collapse, whether violent, or gradual."

The first stage is "sensorimotor," which means to explore the world through the senses, not through genetics. This is the stage of newborns to two-year-olds.

Piaget's second stage is the "preoperational stage," for children ages two to seven. This stage involves learning through discovery and experiential learning (i.e., through experiences in one's environment). Through trial and error, children begin to better understand their own capabilities and limitations. In some cases, a child's aptitude—or lack thereof—will lead to physical or emotional harm. These experiences will be interpreted either positively or negatively by the child, which in turn will affect the child's future decisions. Experiential learning will provide opportunities to either relieve or reinforce fears within the child.

Piaget's third stage, experienced by children from seven to eleven years of age, is known as the "concrete operational stage." Again, something that is concrete is tangible and is typically associated with one's environment. This is the stage in which a child begins to exhibit logical thought (understanding of rules) and apply logic to physical objects. For example, if you pour the same amount of water into two glasses, one taller, the other shorter but wider, the child will likely tell you the taller glass contains more water (if the understanding of conservation has not been taught, learned, and understood). "Conservation" in this case refers to the ability to determine that a certain quantity will remain the same despite the adjustment of container, shape, or apparent size.

The last of Piaget's four stages is the "formal operational stage," in which abstract thought beyond the here and now is emphasized. This stage applies to children eleven years of age and older.

Most educators and psychologists will agree that the most critical stages in a child's development are ages birth to three and again from three to seven. This is when the brain develops most quickly.

By the time children enter the formal operations stage it is expected by those who work in early childhood education, that the foundation for learning has already been firmly established, a learning scaffold has been built. It is at this stage and age that most students are able to fill in gaps and build upon what they already know.

Sensorimotor Stage	Preoperational Stage	Concrete Operational Stage	Formal Operational Stage
0–2 years old	2–7 years old	7–11 years old	11 years and older
Exploring the world through the senses.	Learning through discovery and experience.	Logical thought applied to physical objects.	Abstract though beyond the here and now.

To argue on the basis of nature, one would have to openly admit that genetic foundations are only somewhat important and children can still thrive on the basis of heredity and genetic gifts once they get through the first three stages of their development.

While we have made some progress in education since the Coleman Report, I still find the study interesting. It became quite clear to me that environment does affect academic success in students, however, not necessarily for the reasons deduced by the report. If you accept the premises of the Coleman Report, it could be argued that sending an economically disadvantaged child to school would have no point. We certainly know this is not the case!

The population sample was located in the District of Columbia and included participants of lower socioeconomic status. The Coleman Report might have us believe that no child in D.C. or from any other lower income urban setting would ever amount to anything. Again, we know this is far from the truth. Many students come from disadvantaged backgrounds and become stellar members of society. So what differentiates the students who "make it" and those who don't?

For students who live in poverty, test scores, academic achievements, and graduation rates are significantly lower than those in traditional American suburbs. The Coleman Report suggests that academic achievement is lower because it is not valued and it is not a priority for many of the students in those school districts.

In this regard, I happen to agree with the findings. However, I believe there is an even deeper explanation worth considering. Students who live in lower socioeconomic communities face very tough conditions each day. Many children who live in inner-city communities are victims of poor nutrition, dilapidated housing, and irregular sleep patterns. In addition, these areas often include high crime rates, which causes children to fear the world around them.

Abraham Maslow's hierarchy places physiological and safety needs as the two most basic human areas of human need. Both physiological and safety needs are primitive and trigger a survival instinct. Right above basic safety needs is the need for love and belonging. Data shows that children growing up in inner-city homes have a higher rate of single-parent households than children who grow up in the suburbs, according to studies presented by the *Los Angeles Times*, the Heritage Foundation, as well as U.S. Census data.

The lack of an intact family can place a greater physical and emotional burden on single parents and can cause them to take their frustration out on their children. Furthermore, growing up in a single-parent household can create a sense of abandonment in children, whether they can articulate that feeling or not. These are factors a child must face every day, before he or she steps foot into a classroom.

The notion of esteem, which includes personal achievement, does not find its place in Maslow's hierarchy until after the first three most basic areas of need are met, at least to a significant degree. Students growing up in an inner city environment lives in fear. They are not worried about what college they will get into; they are worried about whether or not they will survive the next day. Students living in poor, urban, environments do not consider their potential, or even fear potential, because all they can focus on is what is actual. In their actual state, they are hungry, they are concerned for their lives and their safety, and they are concerned about who cares about and for them. Fear guides a more primitive behavior and their fear will focus on basic survival needs, not school, and in many cases, rightfully so.

Like most scholars, while I don't discount the importance of heredity, too much of what we know to be true about developmental psychology, education pedagogy, and instructional delivery centers around a child's learning environment. A child who lives in fear cannot progress through Maslow's hierarchy to a state that is conducive for learning. A child who lives in fear cannot work on what he or she wishes to become because the child is preoccupied with survival. I firmly believe that if we took any child living in extremely poor conditions and provided that child with the basic necessities, guaranteed the child's safety, and gave the child authentic and genuine love that he or she was able to recognize as such, that child could immediately move on and begin to develop a sense of potential. The child, living in the absence of fear, would be able to embrace learning moving toward Maslow's self-actualization.

PHILOSOPHY AND AMERICAN EDUCATION

Four major philosophical perspectives have considerably influenced formal education in the United States: idealism, realism, pragmatism, and existentialism, as discussed in the previous chapter. Interestingly enough, not one of the four was exclusively designed with the academic profession in mind. Principle philosophic approaches were created by many well-known historical figures such as Socrates, Plato, Aristotle, Hegel, Thoreau, Augustine, Kant, Aquinas, Dewey, Locke, Hume, Nietzsche, Sartre, Descartes, and of course, many others.

These foundational philosophic views were then used by the likes of Froebel, Harris, Butler, Pentalozzi, Broudy, Wild, and others, to design and guide academic instruction for students in the classroom. Each of the four perspectives reflects the period in which they were created and have the societal values of that era embedded within them. Of the four perspectives—idealism, realism, pragmatism, and existentialism—the former two are traditional and the latter two are contemporary.

In addition to classical realism, realism is also often applied to the field of education, as it was by Pestalozzi, Broudy, and Wild, in which educators begin instruction teaching about concrete objectives that offer specific sensory feedback. Over time, and through understanding of the basics, instruction can then begin discussing more abstract concepts. Realism and realists find value in all subject matter, including arts and sciences; although they do place a high value on the "3 Rs"—Reading, Writing, and Arithmetic.

In terms of education and curriculum, pragmatists encourage students to focus on critical thinking. They want their students to ask questions, be skeptical, and encourage them to dispute the findings of others. In many schools today, we ask students to consider what areas are of interest to them and then encourage them to actively engage themselves in those fields.

> An expanding sense of "other" changes who we are, most importantly for children, what we imagine we can be .
> —Dr. Maryanne Wolf

Although none of these four philosophies are rooted in education, they do possess profound perspectives and approaches for our education system. How we learn, and our philosophy on learning, is just as important as what we learn and what we are taught by others. Learning helps shape actions, and whether we believe there are universal or absolute truths, or whether or not human existence is a matter of perspective; or whether or not our world is constantly changing and we must constantly adapt to changes; or whether or not individualism and self-fulfillment should be the goal of human experience, one thing is certain...learning does not occur in a vacuum. The world around us has cause and effect consequences, and how a student is taught in school, has just as many consequences as what they are taught.

There is no doubt that idealism plays a huge role in education even today. Something as simplistic as a bubble test, or any objective testing measure, requires students to review the list of possible pre-established answers. Educators are asking students to select one right answer among many other incorrect or alternative options. An educator who aligns his or her curriculum under an idealist framework opts to create lessons that highlight humanistic elements related to culture, history, language, and mathematics, while at the same time deemphasizing or reducing the importance of the sciences, which focus on cause-and-effect types of relationships.

Again, how we learn is incredibly important. Since learning doesn't occur in a vacuum, and our environment shapes our understanding of the world around us, it only makes sense that we pick up on lessons that are most relevant to our lives in the moment. Whether we are comfortable or willing to accept this position is a contentious debate. For example, I would argue that a kid on the street will develop an aptitude for drug dealing, hustling, fighting, and so on, because these skills are required for survival in his particular environment. For other youth, even the thought of engaging in such behaviors could create a level of fear and anxiety because other environments have different demands.

What a person fears and the subsequent behaviors based on those fears create a relationship governed by environmental needs and objectives.

HOW DO CHILD ABUSE AND NEGLECT
IMPACT A CHILD'S FUTURE?

As discussed briefly in the chapter on the medical validation of fear, child abuse and neglect are absolutely devastating and disgraceful. Children look to adults for safety and security and to rob them of these basic needs is inhuman. What is even more disturbing is that in most cases, victims know their perpetrators. "Nearly 80 percent of perpetrators of child maltreatment were parents, according to NIS-3 data from 41 states. Another ten percent were other relatives of the victim." (Aldridge and Goldman, 2007)

The data indicates that nine out of every ten victims were abused by the very people whom they should undoubtedly trust the most and people who should have the greatest interest in their safety and security. For this reason, it should be clear why abuse and neglect have such an adverse impact on kids who are victimized. If you can't trust your parents and your family, whom can you trust?

As a result of child abuse and neglect, "children end up suffering from a myriad of maladaptive, antisocial, and self-destructive behaviors and thoughts by trying to cope with the abuse, by trying to understand the situation and why the abuse is happening." (Aldridge and Goldman, 2007) It cannot be stressed enough that when children are the victims of abuse and neglect, they are robbed of their innocence and their childhood. They live in perpetual fear. Often times, these acts stunt future development, lead to long-term psychological problems, and even pathological behavior.

Consider the importance of relationships to human existence. Friendships are built on a foundation of trust. Partnerships with a spouse are built on a foundation of trust. The positive relationships we have in the workplace are generally built upon a foundation of trust. Children who have been abused, especially by people close to them, find it hard to trust others. Their fear then manifests itself in many maladaptive behaviors. Until a person is able to recognize, understand, and manage his or her fear, it will be hard to feel a sense of security or move beyond that point on Maslow's hierarchy. Until he or she is able to feel secure, it may not be possible to build positive, loving relationships that require mutual trust with another.

One reason gang activity is so prevalent in poor urban communities is that such groups provide protection and a sense of belonging to young people. Youth who join gangs view the group as a means of survival, even though they know there are serious risks involved. Well-adjusted children who are loved and have a secure sense of belonging don't join gangs. Joining a gang is a maladaptive behavior that manifests itself because of fear.

In academic settings, it is important that administrators and teacher be aware of incidents of abuse. If school leaders are aware a student has been abused, it should be incumbent upon them to go above and beyond to help a student develop a sense of security, care, and love, of which that youngster has been robbed. It will also be important to make sure that a student who has been abused is protected from any type of bullying or other antisocial behavior that could further harm his or her sense of security.

I would be the first to admit that there is only so much our schools can do. Collectively, however, stopping abuse is a societal obligation that we must accept. If we don't, this anti-social, maladaptive behavior will more often than not become a generational occurrence. To prevent generational abuse, and to help those who have experienced abuse, as a society, we need to take on the problem aggressively and rationally.

First, those who commit abuse need to be punished swiftly and severely. Children who have been abused need to be aware that the perpetrators have been punished severely so the young ones can begin to develop a sense of safety and security in their home environments. This is, of course, often beyond a school's scope of control, though teachers and counselors may certainly become aware of domestic abuse in their students.

Next, children need to be surrounded by those who genuinely care about their welfare and express an interest in them as people. Children need very individualized, positive support and attention to offset the abuse and mistreatment they have experienced. This is not an easy or quick fix. It requires a strong and authentic commitment to the child. Schools and teachers can provide a sense of belonging and care to help students cope with difficult situations. Once a child's *actual* needs are met, he or she will begin to develop *potential* needs, which in turn will lead to more positive development.

Schools must also aim to stress and model positive behaviors and aim to reduce maladaptive or distractive behaviors that students may exhibit as a result of their experiences being abused. Schools need to continue to open students up to pro-social expectations, which foster values consistent with societal norms. In doing so, it will help the students better understand what is right and wrong and direct them toward actions that will result in their success as members of society.

Lastly, I would recommend that students who have been victims of abuse undergo extensive counseling, if and when teachers or school officials become aware that children have been victims of abuse. Since environmental factors significantly impact a child's ability to engage in education, I would be a proponent of public funding to support any such initiatives. I would also seek financial remediation from perpetrators to offset those costs. Counseling should focus on recognizing what has occurred, why it was wrong, and how it made the child feel, so the child can learn to move on. Children and young people must learn to recognize, understand, and manage their fears if they can ever be expected to overcome them.

There is no doubt that undoing or minimizing the damage done is not easy because of how fear, and experience with fear, shape behavior. As Aldridge and Goldman pointed out in their work, abuse does not just affect a child for a moment; it can have a lasting impact. So long as children are afraid and behave in accordance with their fears, they will allow their fear to manage them. Conversely, children who are able to recognize, understand, and manage their fears will be able to manage their own actions and their own destiny. Managing fear is empowering; even if it stems from tragedy or adversity.

THE CHALLENGES OF CLASSROOM MANAGEMENT

Classroom management is one of the most important topics today in the field of education. How children act or behave at school is often a consequence of how the classroom is governed. To achieve the best from students, it is incumbent upon the classroom teacher to create a quality-learning environment that is conducive to learning. From a teacher's point of view, it would be saying, "To obtain their best, we have to give them our best." However, there are differing perspectives with regard to order and classroom management. The two prevailing perspectives currently at the forefront is the notion of heteronomy, which is being governed by others, and autonomy, which is the belief of being governed by one's self. (Aldridge and Goodman, 2007).

Within the context of education, these differing perspectives carry with them perceived advantages and disadvantages. The behavioral psychologist, B.F. Skinner, a proponent of heteronomy, studied the effects of positive reinforcement, negative reinforcement, and punishment, related to human behavior.

Autonomy, on the other hand, is designed to help students become independent decision makers and get to the point in which they can appropriately govern their own behavior. Autonomic classroom management is conceived to help students learn about the morality of their choices and seek to make appropriate decisions. In order to do this, Piaget recommended sanctions of reciprocity which include: temporary exclusion, calling the student's attention to the consequence of his or her action, depriving a student of what he or she has misused or abused, and restitution.

Either approach, heteronomy or autonomy, is rooted in fear. When teachers employ a heteronomous approach, they are managing through fear. They are using their power and authority to demand that students change their behavior. With the autonomous approach, teachers also manage through fear. By requiring students to consider the morality of their choices through sanctions, they are discovering a greater sense of self. A student is not made to fear authority, but rather, respect others. Each sanction is designed to help students reflect on their behavior, understand what they did, and empower them to make better choices moving forward.

Despite the many developmental advantages I see with the autonomous approach, I am not entirely opposed to using heteronomous methods. As previously noted in the discussion of political science, fear can be a very motivating tool. Depending on the students or type of students, it may be more appropriate to use the heteronomous over the autonomous approach. However, because I believe that managing through fear is more effective in the long-term, than managing by fear, I simply would not recommend making a habit of it.

Within the context of the METUS Principle, managing *by* fear is, through some means, establishing an enforcer, someone who holds a higher place and wields a degree of power or authority. Such an environment is one in which a person must answer to another for his or her actions.

On the other hand, managing *through* fear requires a system of introspective reflection. It helps people determine who they are and who they want to be. It helps them understand that their actions shape them and encourages them to make more positive choices to mitigate fear and move toward their goals.

Determining which method to use will depend on two primary factors. Teachers should ask themselves:

- What are my goals as a teacher for my students?

- Am I trying to get them to be independent and productive members of society who are capable of making decisions based on a solid foundation of knowing what is "right and wrong" or am I trying to manage their behaviors because they struggle with the capacity to effectively make appropriate decisions?

If a teacher has a student who is unable to regulate his or her behavior in an autonomous classroom environment, the child may have deeper psychological issues and unresolved fears that hinder the student in managing his or her behavior in a positive way. Helping a child recognize, understand, and manage his or her more immediate fear will be necessary to help the student better manage his or her behavior in a positive manner.

- What is my personal perspective with regard to discipline and classroom management?

Some teachers have a personal bias and feel more comfortable using one method over another. There remains a basic tenet in education: teachers teach what they know. If teachers know fear by fear, they are likely to employ a more authoritarian approach. If teachers know fear through fear, they are likely to employ a more autonomous approach. It comes down to a choice to have power over others or empower others.

FEAR ON THE PART OF TEACHERS

A common source of anxiety (or fear) among teachers is the pressure to cover all of the content in the curriculum within a specified time frame (usually a semester or academic year). There are two distinct philosophical approaches when it comes to instructional delivery: constructivism and objectivism.

To say that a common source of anxiety among teachers is the pressure to cover the content in the curriculum within the semester of school year is an understatement. It has been my experience that there are two primary camps who have a difference of opinion in this arena. One group is committed to evidence-based practices that center on direct and explicit instruction—

the objectivists. Proponents of direct instruction methods are concerned with meeting grade-level proficiency expectations, which align with various state and national standards requirements. This camp relies on ongoing assessments, benchmarking, and standardized testing as a means to gauge success (or failure), based on a set of concrete learning expectations. In many ways, Socrates himself can be considered one of the most distinguished early objectivists.

The second camp is committed to a personal learning approach—the constructivists. In a constructivist approach, students create meaning in their world through a series of individual constructs. Protagoras, in competition with Socrates, was one of history's earliest constructivists. Protagoras claimed, "Each man is the measure of all things." In doing so, a person is able to construct his or her own knowledge and one must only have an opinion, and argue reasons in favor of it, to possess knowledge.

If Protagoras is correct, then no one can be mistaken about anything. This underlying approach in many ways is similar to the constructivist view, as well as humanism, although constructivism has come a ways in two millennia. Modern-day constructivists do promote the scientific method and evidence-based practice. An element of the constructivist model is inductive reasoning, or induction, which is reasoning from a specific case or cases and deriving a general rule. It draws inferences from observations in order to make generalizations.

In education, students will often gravitate toward one approach or the other. I believe they do so in part due to fear. Objectivist students like explicit, systematic teaching. Such teaching methods follow rules, are prescriptive, and predictive. Objectivists gravitate to such areas as mathematics and the physical sciences.

On the other hand, constructivists are more spontaneous and abstract in their thinking. They favor the arts and social sciences. In either case—objectivist or constructionist—we fear things that are new, are difficult, set us up for failure or ridicule, or all these things. We will experience anxiety or fear if what is being taught is not aligned with our learning style preference.

Using the inductive model requires more time because it is a multistep process and is a personal experience for each student. Like Protagoras in ancient Greece, students are encouraged to *discover* knowledge rather than *receive* it. Students begin with observation, analyze facts and patterns, make inferences based on what they have observed and analyzed, and finally perform testing so they are able to confirm their findings. Those who support constructivist learning and support the use of inductive reasoning in the classroom, argue that the aim of education is not to program students and transfer information during their schooling. Rather, education is supposed to produce capable and independent thinkers who are able to contribute to society. They ague that constructivism helps students learn to think critically about things and question their environment in a more scientific manner.

I believe that a balanced approach to instruction is using the appropriate approach at the appropriate place and time. However, from my experience in consulting, I believe that administrators and teachers tend to gravitate to the philosophy that is most comfortable to them, not necessarily what the students need or would benefit them the most. I also believe that, in cases an improper approach has been applied, it has been done on the basis of fear.

For example, when teaching students basic foundational skills, such as reading, it makes sense to use a defined methodology that is both comprehensive and linear. Direct instruction promotes learning through scaffolding, and as students build upon previous knowledge, they are able to remove the scaffolds because they have built a solid structure.

One of the best subjects to discuss the benefits of direct instruction, in my opinion, is reading. Reading requires teachers to teach phonemic awareness and phonics, word recognition and spelling, vocabulary and morphology, grammar and usage, listening and reading comprehension, and speaking and writing.

My view of objectivist versus constructivist instruction has been heavily influenced by the work of Dr. Maryanne Wolf. In her book, *Proust and the Squid*, she illustrates that human beings are not genetically wired for reading. If you drop a child born in New York City off in Mexico, he or she will learn to speak Spanish in order to communicate and live in that society. We have a genetic predisposition to learn speech and we do so at a young age.

If you give a child shapes, even if not explicitly taught the concept of pairing, a child will be able to recognize like objects and pair them. We have a genetic visual predisposition.

Now, if you never teach a child to read and even if you give the child thousands of books, the child will never learn to read. Dr. Wolf's work goes on to explain the evolution of reading and how it came to be a part of the human experience. Based on her work, I believe that the most effective way to teach reading, and any novel concept, is through explicit instruction. For many teachers, this is not easy.

As previously mentioned, a teacher teaches best in the area with which he or she is most familiar. If a teacher has not been educated, in great specificity, how to teach reading to students, it will be extremely difficult for that teacher to explicitly teach reading to his or her students. If a teacher who does not possess a strong background in reading, is asked to teach reading in a sequential, scaffolded, explicit manner, it could cause significant anxiety for that particular teacher.

Instead, it may make sense for teachers to apply a more constructivist approach. They are able to take what they do know of reading and help students construct their learning. In many traditional, constructivism approaches, a teacher will have some whole group and small group discussions, but for the most part, students are encouraged to learn to read by reading. As a teacher teaches basic skills each day, the students' understanding of basic skills improve, and over time, they can practice what they have learned and become better readers. There is only

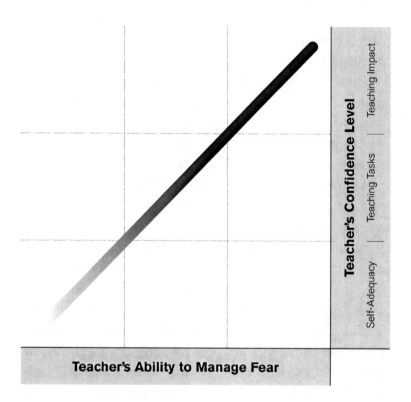

minimal scaffolding involved, but in this example, since the teacher only has a limited understanding of teaching reading his or herself, a constructivist approach is more comfortable for the teacher. In this case, it is the teacher's own fear set the limits for employing the most effective approach for students.

Conversely, fear can also affect a teacher that has a traditional objectivist philosophy. Again, consider reading. Once children have learned to read, they can then read to learn. A constructivist philosophy is a great way to introduce students to a wide array of materials and foster their love of learning. Some teachers rely exclusively on explicit instruction, and over time, "drill-and-skill" practice can turn into "drill and kill" if a teacher is not careful.

Students instinctively pick up on the fear(s) and insecurity of their teachers. Such fears are then internalized by the students and may elicit increased fear on their side. Eventually, it becomes a vicious circle that results in little teaching and little learning. However, teachers can prevent this cycle by recognizing their own limitations, understanding how best to overcome those limitations, and effectively managing their instruction time and their classrooms. Similarly, they can become more tuned in to and aware of these tendencies and help students do the same.

Students who have learned the basics have developed the capacity to become independent learners. They are often eager to learn information that is of interest to them, and if encouraged to do so, teachers can help students realize their fullest academic potential. However, some teachers are uncomfortable with the constructivist approach and lack the creativity to develop lessons that allow for greater student exploration. Again, we teach what we know and if teachers have been primarily exposed to a direct instructional approach, they will have difficulty presenting lessons in a constructivist manner.

Again, I believe there are a time and a place for each approach. When teaching novice learners, with limited-to

-no background in a particular subject area, teachers should be encouraged to develop their ability to teach using an objectivist philosophy, grounded in direct instructional techniques. Conversely, teachers who have advanced learners in their classrooms who have mastered the basics, should be encouraged to become creative and utilize a more constructivist approach.

Teachers should not be limited to their own comfort level, but rather, they should employ instructional methods that are in the best interest of their students. This requires teachers to recognize, understand, and manage their own fears, which can also be described as their instructional strengths and their instructional limitations.

Teachers and students alike are experiencing true fear—fear of survival and lack of safety—due to shootings, muggings, being physically overpowered by students, and so on. Added stress comes from lack of job security, now that teachers unions are less prevalent.

As the great American philosopher and education pioneer John Dewey said, "The path of least resistance and least trouble is a mental rut already made. It requires troublesome work to undertake the alternation of old beliefs."

CAN THE CONCEPT OF FEAR BE APPLIED TO TRADITIONAL EDUCATIONAL THEORIES? IF SO, HOW?

According to Aldridge and Goldman in their book, *Current Issues and Trends in Education*, "Some of the historical and current theories that have influenced education are Gesell's (1925) maturational theory, Piaget's (1952) constructivist theory, Freud's (1935) psychoanalytic theory, Skinner's (1974) behaviorist approach, Vygotsky's (1978) socio-historical approach, Gardner's (1983) multiple intelligences theory, and Bronfenbrenner's (1989) ecological systems theory." While the theories themselves do go into detail, they all provide their own unique and distinct features.

For example, Gesell's maturational theory considers any difficulties a child experiences to be found within the child. In other words, problems are a result of nature, genetics, personality, and other internal factors. Conversely, Skinner's behaviorist theory emphasizes the role of one's environment. When comparing these first two directly, they could be seen in the context or framework of the "nature versus nurture" argument.

Psychoanalytic theory per Freud would have us believe that any problems that we have are due to an unconscious process. It also would stress that a child's, or even adult's, problems are related to their interactions with their parents, especially maternal interactions.

Piaget's constructivist theory tells us that development occurs from the inside out and that through the interactions one has, knowledge is socially constructed through relationships.

The socio-historical approach introduced by Vygotsky gives us the notion of the "zone of proximal development" and culture and language as driving factors in one's development.

Bronffenbrenner's ecological systems theory discusses human development through microsystems, mesosystems, exosystems, and macrosystems.

Lastly, the multiple intelligence theory offered by Gardner provides us with the idea that we all may learn differently, but in eight primary ways: mathematically, linguistically, musically, visually, spatially, kinesthetically, interpersonally, intrapersonally, or as a naturalist. While most of us can learn through all eight, we typically show a preference for one or three avenues, which provide us with our dominant learning tendencies.

Aldridge and Goldman are quick to point out flaws with the current theories used in education. There are three that are highlighted as primary concerns. First, each of the aforementioned perspectives is decades old and all were created by "dead, white, Western, men." The theories themselves leave out significant details that are important when considering them within the context of education. They were not designed to address issues in education, but instead, were used within the context of psychology. If we were to consider both the details, and professional arena, we may reconsider their usefulness. Nor do any of the theories mentioned consider feminist, critical, or post-modern perspectives.

Interestingly enough, although these theories lack specific detail within the context of education and have serious gaps that have been recognized over time, they have been influential in shaping today's educational system. As a society, we have taken elements of these theories and constructed a megasystem. Even the legislation that has and is directing education was developed using the theoretical frameworks given to us by these "dead, white, Western men." Collectively, these theories do provide a considerable amount of valuable insight that is truly worth considering during educational decision-making processes.

In keeping with the theme of this book, each of these theories can be reduced to a single common denominator and discussed within the context of fear. Our basic survival instinct is driven by fear. We have a basic tendency to fear that which we don't know until our experiences give us reason not to. If we never learn not to fear something, or if we have negative experiences that confirm or validate our fear, we will remain afraid. Again, this is a self-preservation, survival instinct.

Thus, maturational theory is simply describing an individual who has either not been exposed to various environmental stimuli, causing that person to remain fearful, or the individual has experienced environmental conditions that have reinforced the fears, whether the person can consciously remember the experience or not.

Psychoanalytic theory would have us believe that any problems we have are due to an unconscious process. It also would stress that a child's, or even an adult's, problems are related to interactions with their parents, especially maternal interactions. Again, this philosophical approach is consistent with a person's innate predisposition to fear; and as such, the underlying cause and effect and correlation-based explanations that can be offered for both maturational and behavioral-based theory still apply. Every interaction we have had with another person or experience we have in our environment, is a determinate factor of our actual self. Our actual self is the product of a collective set of variable factors (experiences) that shape who we are, whether we are consciously aware of it or not, based on fear.

Constructivist theory tells us that development occurs from the inside out and that knowledge is socially constructed through relationships. In other words, our innate fear exists. An external encounter either confirms or reduces that fear, and future actions we take are a result of what we have previously learned in a particular situation. Over time, we learn to generalize and our response to external stimuli becomes nearly automatic until we come across a novel situation.

The socio-historical approach gives us the notion of the "zone of proximal development," with culture and language the driving factors of one's development. Across the world, children are raised in different cultural environments, religious environments, and academic environments. Despite the differences in environmental factors, a child's "zone" will influence learning.

The zone of proximal development is an artificial manner of addressing fear. Within each culture or environment, people are often taught morals, values, customs, and traditions, which help them manage their fear. Stories have traditionally been passed down from generation to generation to help deal with many of life's most challenging or important aspects. This is done to alleviate fear and teach lessons important within that culture, many of which mean survival.

A person's culture may address the potential self as a means of shaping the actual self. In some ways this is analogous with the notion of "self-fulfilling prophecy." A "zone" will help a child recognize, understand, and manage his or her own fear to meet certain cultural expectations. However, it is up to the individual to ultimately accept or reject what is being taught. A child who is taught not to fear the dark, may still fear the dark, if he or she is not able to recognize, understand, and manage that particular fear. As such, a zone may influence development, but it cannot control it in an absolute sense.

Ecological systems theory allows fear to be described on the basis of initial experiences, or through a combination of experiences over time.

Lastly, the multiple intelligence theory provides us with the idea that we all may learn differently. It rightfully demonstrates that we do not all have the same aptitudes, interests, or skills, but we all possess ability. We gravitate toward some things more than others, but we all have the ability to learn. This perspective is not only comforting, but also helps people better understand themselves and strive to further develop their natural skills and tendencies.

Based on research in neuroscience and medicine, I do believe that people can be born with certain genetic predispositions toward learning. Operationally, the brain performs different functions in different areas, and some children exhibit dominant characteristics at a very early age.

While I don't for one minute doubt that some people have a genetic predilection for learning, I refute the notion that a person can be born incapable of learning something. Some endeavors may require considerably more effort than others, but nonetheless, I do believe we are capable of learning outside of our dominate trait comfort zone, with the exception of a small percentage of individuals with severe cognitive or physiological disabilities, approximately three to five percent of the overall population.

What limits a person's ability to succeed is his or her own fear; both real and projected. For example, let's consider the notion of right-brain and left-brain strengths. People who are deemed "right-brained" are said to possess creative strengths, while those who are considered "left-brained" are said to possess analytic strengths. It may be easier for a "right-brain" people to think creatively, but that does not preclude them from learning analytic skills. Similarly, people who are "left brain" certainly can learn to develop creativity. The two tendencies are certainly not mutually exclusive. However, no one wants to struggle or feel incapable. We all want to feel gifted and empowered. As a result, it is easier to gravitate toward those subjects at which we excel and excuse those that require more effort.

It is our own fear that limits us from achieving more. It is our own fear that gets in the way of giving a new skill our best effort. On some level, we are afraid that if we put in the effort, it may very well be for naught, so we tell ourselves we "can't" do something. This is entirely not the case. Although something may be more difficult for us to learn and may require more effort, we can learn new skills. The true question becomes: Are we willing to recognize our fear, understand our fear, and manage our fear, so that we can overcome it and better ourselves and accomplish our goal?

SELF-ACTUALIZATION TO MANAGE FEAR

In 1969, Frances Fuller conducted a study centered on teacher concerns. By analyzing the responses from hundreds of teachers, Fuller was able to determine that teachers' concerns (or fears) varied depending on various stages of professional experience. Using teacher responses, Fuller mapped out seven distinct stages, each of which included a range.

The most basic stage was "teacher concerns." Teacher concerns ranged from self-adequacy to teaching impact. Teachers in the self-adequacy stage are focused on survival. This comes as entirely no surprise, because as new teachers, primitive instinct dominates their conscious state. They pay close attention to performing well when their superiors are around, making a favorable impression on others, and receiving favorable evaluations, all in an effort to survive.

When teachers are confident in their survival and have a sense of security, they are able to progress into a range identified as "teaching tasks." At the teaching task range, teachers are concerned with issues related to instructional and student discipline. This is an enrichment phase in which teachers look to improve methodology.

Superior teachers are at the highest stage of concern, identified on the continuum as the "teaching impact" stage. At this stage, teachers feel confident in their survival, believe they have developed a quality classroom environment, and are more aware of the overall well-being of each student. Such teachers have recognized their fear, understood their fear, and have managed it successfully. In some cases, teachers in this stage may depart from the rules or norms in favor of reaching a student in a way that is most personalized. Teachers in this range could be described as teachers who are more astutely aware of their students' needs and look for ways to diagnose, motivate, and support, each student according to his or her unique needs.

Teachers who are no longer afraid, for all of the right reasons, are empowered. However, please do not for one minute confuse this state of confidence with arrogance. A teacher who is self-actualized is acting entirely out of the good of his or her students, and not at all for self-serving reasons of any kind. There is a distinct difference between teachers who don't care about the consequences and those who are secure with their effort. Such teachers are able to look past basic curriculum and look at the whole child, not for their own convenience, but entirely for the child's. The teacher may be able to best ask, "What is it that this student needs from me, whatever it is, to help them be the best they can be?" It may be non-academic, in fact, and may include issues related to nutrition, health, emotional concerns, or even addictions.

It is interesting to look at this progression from a teacher's point of view. Of course, a new teacher will likely personalize everything and make their job about themselves. "How am I doing?" "Am I a good teacher?" "What do my boss and my colleagues think of me?" Over time, that egocentric view begins to go away and develop into a student-centric view. A teacher may start asking questions like, "How are my students performing?" "Is this lesson one that my students will enjoy?" "What can I give my students to help make learning a particular lesson easier for them?" There is definitely a progression from "me" to "them."

Over time, a superior teacher takes an even greater leap and begins to personalize learning for each of his or her students. Rather than harboring a "me" or "them" attitude, a teacher begins to think about "him" or "her." What Billy needs from his teacher to be his best, will be different than what Sally needs. Teachers who have learned to manage their fear and reach a state of professional self-actualization can achieve amazing things for his or her students.

HOW DOES MASLOW'S THEORY ON NEEDS
APPLY TO BOTH TEACHING AND LEARNING?

As discussed above, Abraham Maslow was a humanistic psychologist most well known for his hierarchal pyramid outlining human needs in order of importance. Maslow's traditional design outlines five primary needs: physiological needs, safety needs, love and belonging needs, esteem needs, and self-actualization needs. There are other interpretations and illustrations that depict up to eight individualized strata with others falling somewhere in between.

Not only does Maslow's hierarchy aim to explain human actions, but it also has profound implications for both teachers and learners. Every child and every teacher in every school across the country deals with fear. That fear may be actual (school violence) or potential (failing an exam), but it is no doubt there. What any of the people fear at any given time will affect the needs and the decision-making process—both positively and negatively. That is why it is so important to learn to recognize, understand, and manage fear.

Let's for a moment consider a child who attends school but comes from a family living in abject poverty. The child's parents are too poor to own a home and the family has been getting by living in the family station wagon. Because money is tight, the student is offered little food outside of what he or she gets as part of the school's free and reduced lunch program. The student is aware that his or her family situation is not normal, feels very hungry due to lack of food, and is often times afraid of sleeping in the car at night, not to mention not being able to get enough sleep.

Looking at Maslow's hierarchy of needs, it is evident that the child's most basic needs are not being met. The student is undernourished, is afraid as a result of living in the family car, and recognizes that his or her situation is not normal. The child's teacher recognizes that he or she has a hard time concentrating in class and does not appear to show much interest in his or her schoolwork. The teacher is familiar with Maslow's hierarchy of needs and understands that the student is likely to continue to struggle in school until his or her most basic needs are addressed.

Assuming that fear is the principle motivator in human behavior, a person is faced with limited options when faced with difficult circumstances. Children have even fewer options because they are limited to many of the choices made by their parents. Teachers, however, are able to positively or negatively address these fears, and as a result, may be able to help a child manage at least some of them.

If a teacher notices that a student is distracted or disengaged in class, it may be helpful for the teacher to consider the student's environment and family situation. Is the student undernourished? Does the child live in a dangerous environment, either in his or her home or community? Are there any unusual circumstances that contribute to the student's feeling of fear or anxiety at school? Are the child's parents together, are they divorced, or has there been a death in the family?

While school staff is limited to the extent in which they can address basic needs, they do have an obligation to consider the safety and well-being of each of their students. If the parents and school staff have done all that they can do, to the extent to which they can meet the child's basic needs, then they can consider needs further up the pyramid.

In some instances, children are also afraid of their parents' responses to poor grades, of not making the football team, or otherwise disappointing their families. Teachers must also be aware of such dynamics, and perhaps discuss such pressures during parent-teacher conversations.

After basic needs, the next set of needs is psychological. If a teacher is able to see the student as a whole person, and consider outside factors that may impact his or her ability to learn while at school, a teacher may be able to develop strategies to best impact the student in a positive way. This can also be described as a holistic approach to teaching, or "teaching with purpose." For Maslow, the goal of teaching was to produce a happy learner who can grow and eventually reach the point of self-actualization. For a teacher, the goal should be to develop strategies to help learners realize that potential. To reach a point of self-actualization requires a learner to have developed into a strong, confident, healthy, and mature learner. In order for a child, or even an adult, to become a strong and confident, he or she must manage their fear along the way.

SUMMARY

Whether an education professional or a parent, it is important to recognize that school can be a major source of fear in a child's life. A student's fear may be tied to academic performance; both high achievement and low achievement, either of which is connected with self-esteem. High achievers place pressure on themselves, or perceive pressure from others, to maintain a high academic standard. Low achievers face personal embarrassment, frustration, and may be required to do additional work, which can all be a source of anxiety or fear. Students may also be a target of bullying, which impacts how safe they feel in their environment, and whether or not they feel a sense of love and belonging, which can damage their self-esteem.

Teachers and other education professionals also experience anxiety and fear. Whether it is job security, job performance, or wondering whether or not they are having the greatest impact on each and every one of their students, there exist pressures to perform. Oftentimes, the teacher's comfort level plays a role—in other words, how well the teacher manages his or her own fears—will have a great effect on the students and how comfortable they are made to feel in the classroom.

The classic "nature versus nurture" debate is certainly relevant in education. School systems often face challenges that are specific to their geographic and demographic factors. This should not be used as an excuse, but rather accepted as a reality. Kids in inner-city urban environments, versus rural environments, versus the suburbs, have their own set of environmental factors that have either supported or mitigated certain elements of fear over time (and continue to do so each day).

Once we recognize and accept that experiences are unique to each child, although many may be similar as a result of their community and home environments, we can help children move closer toward their ideal, self-actualized selves. We can help them recognize, understand, and manage personal fears that are holding them back and keeping them from reaching that state. If we do, we won't necessarily see a child as a "problem," but rather a child who is afraid and unable to manage those fears effectively.

If we can shift our way of thinking to help students become the best version of what THEY want to be, rather than someone WE demand they be, and if we can help them understand that certain choices lead to more positive outcomes for them, we can change our communities in a positive way, one child at a time.

Very similarly, no two teachers are created the same. Each teacher has had unique life experiences prior to ever stepping foot in a classroom. A teacher is a product of his or her unique personalities, life experiences, and educational experiences. They will also relate to different students differently based on their own uniqueness. All teachers carry with them their own fears associated with teaching, and each teacher will manage those fears differently.

Whether a student, teacher, administrator, or parent, I believe it is important we understand fear, and how fear impacts an academic environment each and every day. It is possible—by recognizing, understanding, and managing fear—to create a positive and productive learning environment in which fear is managed so that students and teachers alike may work on moving closer to their own versions of their ideal selves.

NOTES

CHAPTER FIVE
LEADERSHIP, MANAGEMENT, AND FEAR

Kimberly Krueger's Story:
International Author, Speaker and Professional Coach

For some, the concept of crisis management and conflict resolution, is an academic exercise. Those who study to become counselors, therapists, psychologists, or psychiatrists, spend many years and undergo significant supervision, learning techniques and developing skills to help people overcome difficult circumstances in their lives. For Kim, crisis management wasn't academic – it was very real and affected not only her, but also her family.

For years, Kim was married to a man who wrestled with alcohol addiction. When it was clear to her that her husband's addiction was not getting better, but worse, she realized the tremendous toll it was taking on her family, as well as on herself. She turned to a professional therapist, and in a therapy session, she recalled a moment when she told her therapist that she had no choice but to live the way she was living.

Her therapist responded, "No choice? In life, we always have options. We may not like any of them, but we have them." It was that simple and rather unassuming statement that served as a launching pad for Kimberly. That statement would change not only her life, but tipped the first domino that would start a long chain reaction that would touch thousands of other women who faced similar fears and doubts in their own lives.

It was a question that led her to ask herself, "Am I eliminating options in my mind because I don't like them?" The answer, she would soon come to discover, was yes. She had eliminated her options due to fear—fear of being rejected and abandoned by someone she loved. Despite his addiction, and despite how hard his addiction made life for her and for their family, she still loved him – and she didn't want to be alone.

It would take time, but her therapist was able to help her recognize her fear and to understand that despite her fear, she still had options. Kimberly realized that what she was truly afraid of was being alone. It was during that realization that she made a decision to list all of her options, no matter how scary they were. Some were scary and uncomfortable for her, but she did it anyway. She then rank ordered them from bad to worse. She knew there wasn't a good option, because if there had been, her decision would have been easy for her. Realizing there was not a "good" option available for her, she decided to start with the "best" bad option and then work her way down the list. This forced her to face her fear of being alone head-on.

As she considered what it would be like if her husband rejected her—or worse, left her—she realized that when it came right down to it, she was already alone. The alcohol had taken away the man she loved, and although he was physically present, he really wasn't. He was angry or withdrawn most of the time. His addiction robbed her of the companionship she really wanted or needed and left her alone parenting their children the vast majority of the time.

Understanding the harsh reality of her situation, she was empowered to face reality. "If I already feel alone, then could it really be any worse to actually be alone?" The more she thought about it, the more she became convinced that the answer was, no.

"It has to be better to free yourself from the bond of a lonely relationship than to actually be with someone and have expectations of love and togetherness that go unfulfilled." She decided.

After she recognized and understood her fear, she decided to take action. Although difficult and scary for her, she would implement two of the six options that she had previously excluded because of earlier fear, and eventually, her fear would pass. Now officially alone, she wasn't afraid any longer. She was relieved. With each passing day, life only got better. Kimberly was learning to manage her fear and take control of her situation, her happiness, and her life.

Following her independence, Kim was determined to help her children, and eventually, others like her. She became a facilitator for "Love and Logic," a professional development program aimed at teaching parents positive behavior modification techniques for children. She understood that the behaviors modeled by her and her husband for years were maladaptive and were often imitated by her children. She wanted to learn how to better communicate and model positive behaviors, because she realized that if she expected her children's attitudes and behaviors to change, it would have to start with her. Nine years later, she would become the co-founder of the Women's Influence Network (WIN).

WIN was created to help women discover their purpose, live their passion, and expand their influence so that other women can do the same. Kim discovered the power of owning her own choices and she wanted other women to be able to do the same. Shortly after, she branched off and expanded her reach, becoming a Certified Personal Life Coach and Certified Women's Leadership Coach. These certifications allowed her to start her own company, Kimberly Joy Krueger Enterprises, LLC, specializing in women's leadership. Today Kim continues to operate her coaching business, has become a celebrated author and speaker, and also serves on the International Board of Advisors for the Professional Women's Network (PWN).

As a leadership consultant, I am often drawn to the concept of purpose. I recently asked Kimberly to share with me her purpose, and how she defines her work. Her answer was as follows, "My purpose is to open the eyes of women to see what is hindering their fulfillment and success and ultimately empower them to become extraordinary in relationships, business, and life."

I asked her to share with me her perspective of fear, and the importance of learning to manage fear in one's own life.

"I do not believe it is possible to grow as a person, achieve success, or be happy in life without learning how to manage fear. Fear is a growth-stunter because it limits our beliefs about ourselves and what is possible. It puts a ceiling on happiness because it robs us of our peace."

As an advisor serving on the METUS Project, I asked Kim to assess the value of the METUS Principle as it relates to her work as a life and leadership coach. "Recognizing, understanding and managing fear, both actual and potential, is an incredibly powerful skill! It is paramount that leaders in any capacity have the ability to do this—not only to guide others through the process, but to model the process! Modeling is the most powerful form of teaching.

"Imagine if parents modeled the METUS Principle to their children every day. Most parents make decisions because of fear, instead of in spite of it! But when fear is exposed and faced, we can make rational decisions based on what is truly best for all involved, both now and in the long run...The METUS Principle really opened my eyes to the idea that fear is the most basic motivating factor for human beings. This will change my own work as I attempt to uncover what is in my clients' hearts and minds, and how I help them overcome obstacles in their lives."

* * * * *

If your actions inspire others to dream more, learn more, do more and become more, you are a leader.
—John Quincy Adams

As we look ahead into the next century, leaders will be those who empower others.
—Bill Gates

You get what you work for, not what you wish for.
—J.J. Watt

In business, there is a distinct difference between being a manager and being a leader, either of which can achieve lofty goals. The idea of fear is very important in understanding each. Fear is a very powerful and motivating catalyst and can be used effectively in multiple ways. This section will focus on the difference between being a manager and being a leader, and will also provide real-world examples to help distinguish between the two, using the METUS Principle for illustration.

WHAT IS A MANAGER?
A manager is a person who directs a team or groups of people. "Manager" is a word that typically evokes a sharp

response. One of the assignments during my M.B.A. program was to go out and ask people what they thought of when they heard the word "manager."

The most common responses were:

- Someone who is in control

- Someone with power at work

- Your boss at work

- Someone who manages people to do stuff

Almost no one answered the question in a positive manner. Even body language was negative. I noticed raised eyebrows and hesitation when interviewees answered.

When I heard the word "manager" myself, I thought of someone who was under pressure to perform. Mid-level managers, for instance, have the responsibility of directing the people under them so the people above them are pleased. Another consideration I had of managers was that they likely don't get respect or are liked by others. Their superiors look down on them, but expect them to hand the company the world, while their subordinates see managers as heartless monsters who think they own the employees.

In my opinion and from what I have seen in corporate America, many managers put in long, thankless hours for low to fair pay; very few managers can be classified as rich. I see managers as people who are simply caught up

MANAGEMENT BY FEAR

FEAR

in the corporate shuffle with an ongoing struggle, fighting on (at least) two fronts.

Many managers operate in a constant state of fear. Perhaps they fear their superiors are "out to get them" and their subordinates, those they manage, cannot wait to see them gone. Getting people to "do" something can often feel like herding sheep or a game of dominos, in which people knock them down just after they have gotten a few set up.

WHAT IS A LEADER?

A leader is someone who has authority or influence over others, someone who inspires and can be trusted, and much more, as discussed in depth in my book, *The Pocket*

Guide to Leadership: 9 Essential Characteristics for Building High-Performing Organizations. For my assignment, I also asked a number of people to describe a leader in one sentence. These were some of the most common responses:

- Someone who leads.
- A person people follow.
- A captain or coach.
- The strongest person in the group.
- "Me"

I also recorded body language during these interviews, and often noticed that interviewees seemed to have a more positive stance and demeanor when answering this question. Several interviewees tried to follow up their initial response by mentioning a person they knew or a famous individual, and seemed to expect follow-up questions.

When I think of a leader, I think of people like Jesus, George Washington, Derek Jeter, and Aaron Rodgers, to name a few, and take into consideration what it is that makes people leaders. They are all people who placed burdens and pressures on themselves, who see the value in teamwork, and who lead by example.

In my opinion, leadership does not mean operating in the absence of fear; rather, leadership embraces fear. Being a leader requires individuals to embrace their own fears, as well as the fears of those they aim to lead. The best leaders are those who are not only able to recognize, understand, and manage their own fears, but also do the same for those around them—to collectively achieve a common goal or objective. Leaders assume a burden of caring for others. In my *Pocket Guide to Leadership*, I state, "There are reasons some of become leaders and others do not; for as much as everyone would like to have the perceived benefits of leadership, true leadership requires self-sacrifice."

MANAGERS VS. LEADERS

The difference between managers and leaders can be quite significant. Leaders are people who demonstrate confidence, but not arrogance. They are people others believe in and their actions make others want to follow them. They create a sense of inspiration by sharing their dreams, working hard, showing strength, and making others believe their dream is worth working toward. They don't sit back and direct others, but rather, are out in front.

Most importantly, good leaders reduce fears in their followers. They instill confidence in others and bring out their best. Great leaders reduce fear, reduce anxiety, and reduce apprehension, which is why people are eager to follow. When people are confident in their leader and are unafraid, they are able to give their best for the good of the team or the organization, as well as for themselves.

Quite simply, the difference between a manager and a leader is that a manager tells people what to do and how to do it; a leader shows people how to do it and helps them to do it as well. Because fear is such a powerful motivating force, both good and bad, it can be used to achieve the same desired outcome.

As an example, I would like to point out the leadership and management lessons I learned from my father. He does not seek personal gain nor does he put his success above that of those around him. He goes to work every day as a team player who wants to see his team succeed. Seeing this style and hearing the feedback first-hand really made me understand what it means to be a leader and an effective manager.

MANAGING FEAR AND BEING MANAGED

I feel there is a very clear distinction between an individual managing his or her fear, and a boss or superior managing that person. Individuals make choices for themselves based on their values and their goals, overcoming and managing fear. When others attempt to force or dictate behavior that is inconsistent with what a person would choose to do under normal circumstances, that is managing.

Managing includes elements of manipulation, coercion, or subtle use of force. People managing their fears and a person attempting to manage the fears of others are two entirely different things. I feel the former is healthy and productive, while the latter is unhealthy and destructive.

LEADERS GUIDE THEIR ORGANIZATIONS' SUCCESS

Organizations that have managers usually plug away day to day, and if they grow, they may show small, steady growth. Organizations with leaders rise above the rest. A great example can be found in the airlines industry. Most airlines operate at a deficit and are not very profitable, if at all. Southwest Airlines is different. Southwest is not a unionized company. It is guided by a leader who treats everyone with equal value.

The leader most people associate with Southwest Airlines is the founder, Herb Kelleher. However, leadership at Southwest has not been limited to Herb. At Southwest Airlines, leadership is a core value and keeps people at the forefront of all its decisions. As a result, the people who work for Southwest love their company and feel lucky to be a part of it. They are an example in the industry of how business could and should be.

When you think of sports, perhaps people like Michael Jordan, Derek Jeter, Joe Montana, and Wayne Gretzky come to mind. They are the icons everyone looks up to. However, just because a player has a "C" on his jersey to indicate that he is the captain of the team, it doesn't necessarily mean that star is a true leader. Many of the superstars across sports lead through fear, intimidation, and with a heavy hand. Despite their individual greatness, this is not leadership; it is management.

Through my own observation of sports icons, I have discovered that players like LeBron James, Joe Montana, Ray Lewis, and Derek Jeter are genuine leaders. They are on the field or the court coaching other players in a constructive manner, supporting their teammates, and looking out for them. They lead by example and want everyone around them to be their best for the good of the team.

I have also noticed that some sports icons lead from behind, even some truly accomplished ones. Athletes like Lance Armstrong, Jay Cutler, and even Michael Jordan could be deemed managers rather than leaders. I don't see them as players who are out to help make everyone around them better. They seek to instill fear in those around them, rather than mitigate those fears.

The same can be seen in coaching. Coaching icons like John Wooden, Jim Torre, and Jim Tressel treated their players as men first and athletes second. They looked out for them, treated them with dignity, and encouraged them to be their best. They led with their hearts and not with the stick. Conversely, there have been many coaches who have created their legacy by using the stick. Coaches such as Bobby Knight, Ozzie Guillen, and Nick Saban, use fear and demand action through fear.

In terms of sports leadership, there is no player or coach I respect more than the late John Wooden. His philosophy was so simple, yet so inspired. He made being a great leader look almost effortless because of his ability to bring out the best in his players. He did so by encouraging them to focus on being their best, reducing outside distractions, and as a result, he mitigated their fear. In Wooden's words, "Leadership is listening, observing, studying, and trial and error...don't worry if you are better than everyone else but never cease to be your best." He didn't worry about winning as much as he did about self-improvement.

Winning was a by-product of managing fear and working on becoming the best. Wooden taught his players that if they worked to beat the competition, they wouldn't know when someone or some team better would come along. If a player or team becomes the best at a given point, complacency tends to set in. However, if players work to constantly improve themselves, they can never get complacent because no one is ever perfect and there is always room for improvement.

If you take this approach—improving yourself—you will achieve far more than you originally thought was possible. Another of Wooden's quotes is "There is a choice you have to make in everything that you do, so keep in mind that in the end, the choices you make, make you." Again, what an amazing thought to ponder. You are your actions. It is easy to get a sense of why John Wooden was viewed as such a great leader and motivator. His words are reassuring and reduce fear.

Another great approach to distinguish leaders from managers is expressed by Bill Johnson of Southeastern Michigan Gas. He takes the people and personal values approach, mentioning traits of quality leaders: truthfulness, respectfulness, results orientation, and personal drive. Johnson discusses a major problem he views with today's "leaders," who don't lead or manage—they boss. This approach creates inner problems for business teams and weakens the support system, which leads to the organization falling apart. He states that you can't just tell people what to do; you have to be involved and work with them to reach their desired goals.

It takes involved, hands-on leaders who care about their people and their organizations. Great leaders are selfless in their approach. They are not after personal gain and truly are people who see the big picture, which Johnson explains are some of the reasons people around them are willing to work so hard. He stresses respect and caring and feels that if one leads well, the team will follow and goals will be reached.

LEADERSHIP AND COMMUNICATION

You have likely heard the saying, "It's not what you say, but how you say it."? Let's focus on what this statement means and why it is important in oral communication. When we speak, we use many ways to express ourselves and to get our message across to our listeners. The words we choose, our body language, our gestures, and our facial expressions are all important aspects of communication. Although the words we choose are important, the meaning of those words is also influenced by several other factors: how we say those words and where we place the emphasis.

As listeners, such factors give us insight into the emotions of the speaker and what he/she considers important. It is our job as listeners to use the cues the speaker provides us to correctly understand, or attempt to understand, the underlying message.

Management is secondary after the leadership role has been fulfilled. Management takes the leadership foundation and allows those around the leader to do their jobs with minimal interference. Good managers trust their team and are there not to interfere or instill fear, but to guide when necessary. They help others believe in themselves, and they shoulder a lot of the load to reduce the fears of those they lead. At the end of the day, both managers and leaders can potentially produce the same outcome; but leaders and their team are better off because of the collaborative approach.

You can find inspiration everywhere you look; just keep an open mind. Consider a movie like *Glory*, with Mathew Broderick and Denzel Washington. To me, it becomes abundantly clear that in times of war, true leaders have a few things in common: they are all at the forefront, they put themselves out there, they communicate and listen well, and they lead by example. They overcome their fears for the good of others, and as a result, mitigate those fears.

Inspiring and leading people is all about creating a vision and presenting a clear picture of where you are trying to go. That direction must be explained in a way that resonates with those you are trying to lead and often involves providing people with a clear map of how to get there.

The last key ingredient of a great leader is inspiration. People who are inspired are confident, not afraid. People who are inspired are motivated, not subdued. Leaders inspire their team to reach new heights through a "can do" attitude. More importantly, they are sincere, which is essential when attempting to inspire.

Using the example of an athletic team, a great leader is one who always shows up early for practice, is the last one to leave, carries the team through tough times, avoids placing blame on others, spreads praise around to the team when times are good, and places a heavier burden on their own shoulders when times are rough.

A great leader is always there to offer non-judgmental assistance and earn the respect of those around them because the team knows that individual has the best interest of the team at heart. He or she is a person who is not a "me" person, but a "we" or "us" person. Such individuals want others to be at their best and believe in the capacity of others to become strong, confident, successful, and capable. A leader is someone who puts ego aside for the betterment of the people he or she leads, much like a proud parent.

CORE VALUES TRUMP FEARS

In highly successful organizations, leaders speak of a guiding compass, an emphasis on morality and ethics, or core values. Core values are the driving force that guides an organization in conducting its affairs. Such characteristics include honesty, an emphasis on people, being respectful, individuals who value family time, truthfulness, workers who are results-driven, and also include team members with technical expertise. Core values are about people, plain and simple.

In studying a variety of organizations, I've observed that many people who deem themselves leaders are in truth nothing more than managers. While they may be in positions of authority, they may be managing and running an operation, but they are not leading. This approach is hurting businesses, and it is certainly hurting our society. Managing rather than leading creates internal problems, inefficiency, employees questioning the integrity of the person in charge, and may result in internal battles and lack of productivity.

One of my favorite books is *Wooden on Leadership*, by late coach John Wooden. I was completely blown away by his unique, but extremely insightful, perspective regarding self-improvement. Whether John realized it during his life or not, his perspective on self-improvement embodied a personal quest toward self-actualization. Furthermore, his application from a coaching standpoint defined leadership and how to go about maximizing both individual and team performance.

The first major learning from Wooden's book is my favorite because I believe if we all really took this lesson to heart, not only would the world be a better place, but we would all have a deeper sense of self-worth and accomplishment. Wooden says, "Don't worry if you are better than others, but never cease to be the best that you can be."

So often, we measure ourselves against others. A self-actualized life isn't about going out and trying to outdo everyone you come across. It is about personal growth, pushing yourself to become better, working toward the apex of your ability, and then performing to the best of that ability.

If our approach is only to best our opponents, we really wouldn't be achieving as much as we thought we were. I have learned this lesson repeatedly: someone else will always come along who is bigger, faster, stronger, smarter, or more cut-throat than we are to put us in our place. However, it doesn't matter what others do and our worth shouldn't be based on what others can or can't do.

It is our job to push ourselves to the limit, strive to be the best we can be, fight the battle against ourselves physically, emotionally, and mentally, and never quit working to become better.

I particularly like how John phrased his statement because it speaks to the heart of human tendency, which follows the METUS Principle. He says, "Don't worry..." or in other words, don't be afraid and don't fear. Taking John's words a step further, his words have implications in both the actual and potential sense for an individual.

If I were to paraphrase John, incorporating the METUS Principle, his statement may be amended to say, "Don't worry if you are actually better than others, but never cease to be the best that you can potentially become."

It is important that players, or people in general, do not let fear and hard limit stand between them and their potential. Work is hard, and hard work is harder, which is why people are often afraid of it. If we let our actual fear dictate our behavior and choose not to give our best effort, we will never have the chance to realize our true potential. Wooden realized this, which is why he wanted his players to be their best—and not to worry about being better than others.

The great thing about John's approach, and one of the major reasons he was an incredibly accomplished coach, is that by shifting the focus from external competition to internal competition, he was able to unlock the key to success, which resulted in winning. Because it is harder to constantly fight and compete against yourself than it is to compete against another, John's athletes were always mentally and physically tougher than the people against whom they competed.

Another consequence of this approach was that it allowed his players to be more relaxed. Again, Wooden's approach aligns nicely with the METUS Principle. He was able to help his players recognize, understand, and manage their fears by demonstrating that success comes from within, and not from without. His players competed with confidence because they knew they had prepared themselves to succeed. They were able to keep calm in the face of adversity, because inside, they knew what they had to do and had practiced doing it day in and day out with their coach. They didn't have to work harder or oppress their opponent; all they had to do was correct the mistakes on their end, which gave them a sense of empowerment and control.

LEADERS ARE TEACHERS

Another learning from John Wooden's book was the idea of leaders being teachers. I hadn't given much thought to the nuts and bolts of this statement until Wooden explained it. I obviously know that leaders teach. That is how the next generation learns in our society. I didn't, however, think of a teacher as a leader and a leader as a teacher in the way John went on to describe it. John says, "Don't be misled by titles on a business card or desk ornament; leaders are teachers, plain and simple." He doesn't say, "I'm a born teacher, a born leader, and that made me in to the coach I was." Instead, he takes the approach that in the beginning, everyone is a student. Everyone has to learn and develop his or her leadership skills, even if the person who teaches you along the way is yourself.

John went on to say that teaching and learning were an ongoing process and that he never stopped learning. He also said that in the course of learning, he also learned to teach. He learned to pass on his knowledge and that made him in to a great leader, and being a great leader ultimately made him a great coach. John possessed tremendous abilities, including his gift to coach, to teach, to motivate, to inspire, because he was confident. John was confident, because his approach to self-improvement recognized and understood fear in a way that allowed him to manage it successfully.

FAILURE TO PREPARE

John Wooden also stated, "Failing to prepare is preparing to fail." This is so very true. If you allow yourself to take the easy way out, you are allowing your fear to manage you. If you allow yourself to cut corners, if you are satisfied with giving a second-rate performance at practice, you are setting yourself up to fail. Conversely, if you recognize your fears and understand them, you can begin to manage them.

Often, managing our fear means putting in the time, energy, and effort, that are required to overcome our limitations and our shortcomings. When we put in the time to address our shortcomings, we exhibit growth and improvement, and thus prepare ourselves for success. Players who are honest with themselves understand that a second-rate performance in practice will manifest itself in a game. Therefore, players who are truly at the top give their best at every practice.

Another Woodenism is "Because you can't give 110 percent tomorrow to make up for a 90 percent perform- ance today, you had better make sure you give 100 percent each and every time you set out to accomplish something." I love this quote because so often, we think, "I will hurry in this moment and make up for it the next time around."

STICKS AND CARROTS

Remember the adage, "The carrot is mightier than the stick." Fear is an extremely powerful motivating influ- ence. Because fear does motivate people, many people get caught up in believing that the bigger the stick, the greater the action. While it is true that fear gets people to act, causing people to fear to get them to act also produces unintended consequences, for fear strips them of a feeling of security, belonging, and love, the essential pillars in Maslow's hierarchy.

If you are trying to build a high-performing team, maximize its capacity, and make it sustainable, the stick isn't your best choice. Over time people will become numb to the stick and you will need a bigger stick to get the same effect, and then a larger one, and a larger one. Eventually, people will become less afraid of the immediate, actual consequence, and more afraid with a future potential consequence. When that happens, the stick is no longer effective.

When talking with a number of people about leadership, most don't believe great leaders use "the stick." My father, in particular, told me, "You have to make others share your vision. Make those you wish to lead want to follow you, not by force, but by inspiring them to do so."

A carrot is mightier than the stick because a carrot will not only satisfy our basic needs, it does so by reducing fear. For this reason, carrots are sustainable and allow people to pursue their higher purpose and put more attention on self-improvement.

CREATING A GREAT LIFE

A great life isn't based on any one aspect or any one accomplishment. I know many rich people who are miserable and many poor people who are happy. I know many disabled people who are grateful they are alive and many physically gifted people who are spiteful. I know many smart people who are ignorant and many uneducated people who are wise. The bottom line is there is no universally accepted definition of success.

Living a great life, in my opinion, means working hard in every aspect to be the best you can be at whatever it is you chose to become. Being great means doing the best in a position you actually hold and always working at becoming the best you can potentially become. Being great means that along with excelling at work, you excel at home in your duties as a spouse and parent. Living a great life means you are always working to improve and become better actually so you may realize what you can become potentially. It means that you don't allow yourself to settle and fall into the rut of "the daily grind." Instead, you move along, innovate, and achieve.

In Jim Collins' book, *From Good to Great*, we are told a history of several individuals who founded or built great companies. He also introduces his "the window and mirror philosophy."According to Collins, "Poor leaders look out a window or to outside factors when things aren't going well. However, these same leaders are the ones who preen in the mirror and are quick to take credit when things are going well."

Although Collins never explicitly stated this, the "window and mirror" philosophy could also be used to describe great leaders, as well as poor ones as follows: "Great leaders look out a window or to outside factors when things ARE going well. However, these same leaders are the people who accept blame and look themselves square in the eye, in the mirror, when things are going poorly and tell themselves people are counting on them. They tell themselves they need to perform better because their teams are counting on them."

Great leaders distribute praise and are happy to give credit to others because they possess confidence in their own effort and their own ability. They are not afraid of giving credit to others because they are internally secure. Truly great leaders are also people who don't shy away from blame and aren't afraid to carry the weight of the team on their backs when times are tough, to steer the ship in the right direction.

It would make sense for people to gravitate toward work or activities they truly care about. However, from my observations, this is not often the case. Instead, people let shortsighted goals or a quick dollar opportunity take the wheel and steer their decisions. Before they know it, they find themselves on a path on which they never really wanted to go. Their short-term fear of passing up on what they saw at the time as an easy dollar interfered with achieving future goals and greater passions. In doing so, people move away from a self-actualized state.

If you love your job and you wake up every day eager to make progress, not only does your work not seem like work, you will be more inclined to give it everything you have, day-in and day-out. That is what life is like when you properly manage your fear.

LEADERS LIVE BALANCED LIVES

Clayton Christiansen's work, *How Will You Measure Your Life?* teaches us that balance is essential for mastering our fear: balance between work, study, our faith, our friendships, our families, and our loves. When our life is in balance, everything that important to us is given proper attention. If we neglect any one area, we will still have a lingering fear in our life, whether we are able to recognize it readily or not.

We cannot be at peace when we do not manage our fear. To this end, Maslow's hierarchy is in fact a useful tool in helping us understand how to address and overcome fear in a systematic and balanced way.

When we give ourselves to others in a meaningful exchange, this reduces fear. However, it would be both unreasonable and unwise to wish for a life without fear. Fear, when recognized and managed, helps us make decisions that are consistent with survival and self-preservation. Fear also helps us make sense of our priorities, both short-term and long-term. Fear helps us develop a sense of self and who we want to "be." If we did not fear injury or death, we would take unnecessary and dangerous risks. If we did not fear failure, we would not be motivated to take action to achieve success.

Fear that is recognized, understood, and managed, is balanced. The METUS Principle is consistent with Christensen's approach to living a life that has value and that provides us with fulfillment. Christensen's measure of life is rooted in the framework of self-actualization. When we look back, how will we measure our lives? Did we find the success we had hoped for? Do we have any regrets? Did we manage our fear and find a balance in life? A person who lives in balance will ultimately be able to positively answer these questions. with a resounding "yes."

MY DAD, BRAD PETERS:
THE PRINCIPLE OF MANAGED RISK

I have spent thirty years of my life idolizing my dad, his success, and his accomplishments. My dad happens to be one of the smartest people I know; I also believe I can say this from both an objective and subjective point of view.

He graduated in the top of his class in both high school and college as a straight 'A' student, received a perfect score on his ACTs, and scored in the top 1 percent on his CPA exam, earning him the Elijah Watt Cell Award. Subjectively, I have observed his ability to learn very quickly, across various disciplines and trades. My father has been extremely influential to enhancing my own love of learning.

When I was younger, I often wondered why a person of my dad's intellect and ability wasn't a millionaire many times over. That is not to say he hasn't done very well for himself and accomplished a lot both professionally and personally; he certainly has. Foolishly, I tried to understand my dad's success solely on the basis on financial gains, which I had believed should have been exponentially greater. Shortly after graduating from college, I asked him some very direct questions.

He responded, "Many people who are exceedingly wealthy have not inherited their fortune, and had to face personal and financial failure many times before getting where they are. Many more have tried and never gotten the break they were searching for to amass considerable wealth. Becoming rich and not just comfortable, works best when a person has nothing to lose, and is desperate for a break; or so rich that he or she can afford to take significant risk in the hope that it pays off. I chose to marry young and start a family. As a result, I made a conscious decision to manage my risk and take enough chances to provide a comfortable life for my family, but not too great a risk that I would risk everything I had worked for."

This was a very insightful perspective, but it is not the end of the lesson.

When talking with my mom, I learned that my dad had a number of significant opportunities he turned down when I was growing up, positions that could have made him a millionaire many times over. When those opportunities came up, he turned them down. The question was why?

My mom told me that the positions he could have pursued were all out of state. It would have required him to pull his four kids out of their school(s), out of their community, and away from family, all of whom lived in Wisconsin. The jobs offered would have likely required more work, longer hours, and more time away from his family. It wasn't that my dad was afraid of hard work; it was that he was afraid of sacrificing his family for his job. My dad was the father who attended every football game, every baseball game, every basketball game, and every important event we had as kids, even if it meant running straight from work in his suit and tie to watch us play. In fact, my dad only missed ONE football game of mine ever, and it was because of work. My mom told me it makes him sad to this day.

My father's explicit and concrete decisions placed his family as a priority. He said it not only in words, but in deeds. His idea of self-actualization had nothing to do with becoming rich or having an impressive title; it was about providing a great quality of life for his family. In fact, I asked my mom if my dad ever explicitly ever told her what his career goals were. She told me, "Your father's goal was to make sure he earned enough money to put each of his four kids through college. Along the way, he wanted to make enough money so that you not only had what you needed, but also what you wanted if you were willing to earn it.

Most importantly, he wanted to be a part of his kids' lives, see you grow up, teach you anything that you wanted to learn, and show you every day how much he loved you." She also told me that was her goal, too, and why collectively, they made the decision for her to be a stay-at-home mom.

I truly do not think I will ever be able to express to my parents just how much I love them, and appreciate the decisions they have made for our family. They mastered the concept of balance, and managed risk, and I feel much of what I have learned from life I learned because of who they are. I love you both.

SUMMARY

In my estimation, one of the main differences between managers and leaders is that leaders are more able to recognize, understand, and manage their fears. They are also able to do so for the people they lead. In many instances, managers fear their subordinates, as well as their superiors, and thus are caught between the proverbial rock and a hard place.

Managers are fully capable of recognizing, understanding, and managing their fears, but societal pressures, the group think of "we've always done it that way," and the hierarchical way that many organizations are run, can stand in the way of managers' actually being able to step out of the fear trap and become leaders in their own right.

NOTES

CHAPTER SIX
ECONOMICS AND FEAR

Kim Sponem's Story:
CEO/President of Summit Credit Union

From a very young age, Kim Sponem knew that she wanted to be a business leader. After she graduated from high school, she attended the University of Wisconsin, where she would earn her bachelor's degree in marketing and consumer science.

It was in 1990, following her graduation from the UW, that she would "fall into the financial services industry." In her first job out of college, she worked for the Credit Union Executives Society as Programs and Services Director. Realizing that in order to achieve her dream as a business leader, she would have to begin working her way into management and other leadership roles. In just over a year, she would take a step up the career ladder, accepting a position as Marketing Director for the State Capitol Employees Credit Union. In this role, she was responsible for the overall marketing strategy, including market research, database research, product development, pricing, advertising, media buys, budgets, and training. Kim would also write and implement a marketing plan section under the company's strategic plan.

As marketing director, she was able to demonstrate her ability to be a forward-thinking, visionary, leader, and her efforts were noticed by the Great Wisconsin Credit Union, where she was offered a position as their VP of Marketing and Development. At Great Wisconsin, known today as Summit Credit Union, she would earn two more promotions, and before long, at the age of but 35, Kim was promoted to the company's senior-most executive position, CEO and President.

In her twelve years as President/CEO, the credit union has grown from $210 million in assets to $2 billion. The branch network expanded from 4 locations to 25, net worth grew from 8.5% to 11.5%, and the Credit Union has won dozens of awards for best credit union to do business with, best training programs, best place to work, and many other categories. Summit Credit Union consistently obtains Net Promoter Scores in the 60s, compared to 15% as the average in banks and 30% as the average in credit unions.

Kim's visionary leadership led to the creation of STAR Credit Union, the only kids credit union in the country, because she believes that financial education for youth is very important to helping to improve their financial lives and the communities in which they live.

All this success was achieved as her organization went through seven mergers and two name changes. As a business leader, Kim has received a number of honors including being named among the most 25 most influential people in Madison, WI by *In Business Madison*. This was no small feat when you consider other names included, such as Wisconsin Governor Scott Walker, UW Head Basketball Coach Bo Ryan, and Pleasant Rowland, the creator of the *American Girl* doll, just to name a few.

With an introduction from a mutual friend, Kim agreed not only to serve as a reviewer for my book, but was also willing to sit down for an interview. When I asked her what she thought of the book, she responded, "I found myself agreeing with your premise, particularly as it relates to financial services. Approximately 88% of the economy is driven by consumer confidence and confidence is determined by how secure or safe people feel investing." I asked her to elaborate on that thought – specifically as it related to her role as CEO/President of Summit.

"Our business [as a creditor], and our ability to grow, depends on whether or not people are willing to borrow money for things such as a new home, purchasing cars, or investing in a business. People are typically more willing to accept that type of risk when the economy, and their jobs, are more stable."

In addition to gaining insight on how Kim perceives fear in the economy, I was also interested in her views on how fear and leadership were connected to one another. Although Kim was very humble, she did express that leadership roles are not right for everyone. Being an effective leader requires, at times, the ability to put aside thoughts of what others may think of you.

"A leader has to be willing, when it makes sense, to object to a bad idea or point out potential problems that need to be addressed, for the good of their company."

Kim pointed out that this can be difficult to do for some people. For starters, some people simply do not like conflict, while other times, people are reluctant to offer an opposing view out of fear that their comments may hurt someone else's feelings.

"It is [these] fears that stand in the way of someone's ability to communicate his or her ideas – and in fact, many great ideas every day, by employees everywhere, will go unheard because they were too afraid to share them."

From this statement Kim was able to make a counterpoint that not only do effective leaders learn to manage their own fear, they are also able to help their employees successfully manage theirs. The idea of helping employees manage their fears can be somewhat compli-cated because it is not always easy to identify who needs support, and even when you may notice an employee who may need support or encouragement, it can be challenging to determine the best way to approach a person or offer assistance.

Many of us look up in our company hierarchy and we say to ourselves, "If only I were in charge." What most of us fail to appreciate at times like these is most people struggle when making difficult choices. Most of us prefer to make easy choices, or choices that we believe to be personally advantageous, but leadership requires more than that. Leadership requires leaders to make very difficult choices that have the potential to affect not only themselves, but others as well. Depending on what choices need to be made, and whom a decision will affect, leaders may run the risk of damaging their reputation in the minds of those who will be adversely impacted.

In some situations, a decision will come down to "being liked" or doing what is right. It can be a hard thing to make a decision that will cause others to dislike us, or in some cases, possibly even hate us; but at the end of the day, good leaders are able to get past these fears and ultimately do what is best for their organization. On the surface, this may sound simple, but when you are the person in control of the red button, and the decision rests on your shoulders, the choice may not be as easy as one may think.

When I asked Kim about her own fears, she paused for a moment. Looking across the table she smiled and said, "Throughout our lives, I think all of us have doubts about something at some time or another. We may wonder, am I the right person for this job or, do I have all of the information that I need to make this decision? But I think those thoughts are perfectly normal, whether people want to admit them or not."

Kim also noted that no one gets anywhere in life entirely alone. We all have teachers or mentors who influence us, or people who give us a particular opportunity, and once we get an opportunity, it is up to us to make the best of it. When I spoke to Kim, I got the sense that her ability to manage her fear was driven by her desire to be well informed. Re-reading my notes, I started to pick out common themes such as, "asking the right questions"; who will [this] decision affect and how will it affect them; "having enough information"; "having the right information", and understanding timing in the decision-making process.

While Kim ascended the corporate ladder very quickly, becoming CEO/President by the age of 35, I do not think that her success can be attributed to chance. Instead, I believe that it has to do with her ability to recognize, understand, and manage fear – in both herself and others – in order to have a positive impact on her organization and her team members around her. As a leader, she is concerned about the best interests of those around her and the best interests of her organization. At the same time, she is willing to make tough decisions and take responsibility for those decisions at the risk of what some may think of her.

As a leader, these are two incredibly important qualities. It is isn't enough to simply put aside fears of what others may think of you; it is also about doing what is best for the organization and the majority of those people around you. Making decisions not just when it is easy, but instead, when there is a very complicated and challenging situation, is what differentiates those who are leaders from those who are simply in charge.

* * * * *

As a consumer, you want to associate with brands whose powerful presence creates a halo effect that rubs off on you.
—Tom Peters

Critics of consumer capitalism like to think that consumers are manipulated and controlled by those who seek to sell them things, but for the most part it's the other way around: companies must make what consumers want and deliver it at the lowest possible price.
—James Surowiecki

Economics is the social science that studies the behavior of individuals, groups, and organizations, when they manage or use scarce resources, which have alternative uses, to achieve desired ends. Economics and market forces are based on supply and demand—which in turn, have much to do with the principle of fear. People fear not having enough, or are willing to pay higher prices for resources they believe will run out or become scarce.

The word economy can be traced back to the Greek word *oikonomos,* "one who manages a household." Today, this word includes concepts of "thrift," "direction," "administration," "arrangement," and "public revenue of a state," and it now incorporates the current sense of "the economic system of a country or an area."

I contend that the economy and economics are fueled by fear; and in some cases, what may appear to be the relative absence of fear. From the daily purchasing decisions of the average consumer to trends depicted by the growth or decline by our market exchanges, we see fear manifest itself in our daily decisions.

THE AVERAGE CONSUMER

Earlier in this book, and on the cover, you were introduced to a graphic representation of the METUS Principle. Embedded within the image is a pyramid, which symbolizes Abraham Maslow's hierarchy of needs. As living creatures, we all have needs; but as an intelligent species, our needs have developed in terms of complexity as well. At times, there is a fine line between a person's needs and his or her wants; and in some cases a person catapults that line and the person covets something that is clearly a "want," as opposed to a "need."

There are many ways to explain a "want." Wants fill some purpose for the person acquiring the service or item. In some instances, a "want" makes a person's life or efforts easier in some fashion—or at least that may be how the buyer justifies a purchasing decision, or a robber justifies a theft.

In other instances, a "want" serves as a status symbol and communicates to others an image the acquirer wishes to portray—or at least this is the person's belief.

Successful companies and sales representatives know how to identify needs and wants. Many sales strategies even have a defined term embedded in their interview and meeting process: "the pain point." This term addresses the things that keep people up at night, or "Who gets the call when things go wrong," or the ultimate question, "Whose head is on the chopping block if XYZ fails?"

Authors like Jeff Thull, Robert Miller, and Stephen Heiman, explain "pain points" in a positive and productive manner. If a consumer's fear of not having something outweighs his or her fear of parting with the money, time, or energy, the consumer is more likely to make the purchase.

In many cases, needs and wants are genuine and the consumer has an easy choice. In other instances, an organization or sales professional will assist with manufacturing perceived fear to move a sale forward. Companies walk a fine line between providing products that mitigate a consumer fear and manipulating fear for profit. Marketing and advertising are an extension of the sales process, and operate in a similar vein.

I am often fascinated with marketing and advertising campaigns as I try to determine what message the company, organization, or person, is trying to convey to me to turn my "wants" into "needs."

In terms of marketing and advertising, very few people would argue that the underlying purpose is to "fill a need" and attract consumers to their product to fill the need in question. Yeah, so what? Most of us already know this. However, how many people have really given much thought to how a company attempts to communicate its message and attract prospective customers? The answer may seem obvious to some, but I am guessing it may also come as a surprise.

One article I like to point to, to illustrate my argument, is a short piece written by Joe Constantino in 2011 for businessmarketingsuccess.com. Joe's article, "Again, What is the Purpose of Marketing?" offers three simple objectives that a marketing campaign should accomplish:

- Build awareness, credibility and trust with your preferred prospect or customer
- Facilitate the decision making process of your preferred prospect or customer
- Lower the risk for your preferred prospect or customer to take the next step in the buying process

Now, looking at these three objectives, let's dissect them for a moment down to their lowest common denominator—Fear. Number one, build awareness, credibility, and trust. Earlier in this book, I mentioned that as human beings, we have a natural fear of the unknown. It is our default feeling toward something because we do not have any experience to refute that which we do not know.

When a company aims to create brand awareness, it is working to reduce that fear or anxiety by telling consumers, "Hello everyone...this is who we are... and this is what we can offer you. You can trust us." Creating awareness isn't necessarily attempting to convince a consumer to purchase a product or service; rather, it is convincing people to "buy" the company.

Then there is credibility. Credibility attempts to alleviate a consumer's fear by illustrating why the company can be believed in and is "A-okay." Organizations attempt to establish credibility through testimonials, endorsements, or referrals, which are nothing more than leveraging the credibility, or perceived credibility, of someone with whom consumers may identify (age, gender, common challenge, and so on) or admire. Testimonials, endorsements, and referrals work because another person is risking his or her own reputation, and credibility the person has with you, to tell you he or she stands behind and believes in the company, organization, or person. The assumption is often, "So-and-so wouldn't attach himself / herself to this group if it were bad," which by and large is a fair assumption.

The third word in the first line is *trust*. Trust is big. When we trust someone, we are not afraid of them. We let our guard down and are more apt to accept what he or she tells us. As far as sales are concerned, I am much more likely to buy something readily from someone I trust than someone I have never met, done business with, or someone with whom I have not established a degree of trust.

The second purpose of marketing, according to Constantino, is to "Facilitate the decision-making process of your preferred prospect or customer." What does this exactly mean? Well, basically it conveys the concept of creating an "auto buyer." This is someone who becomes

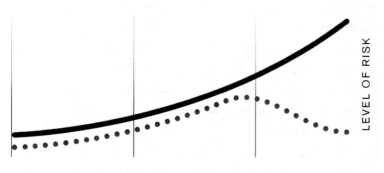

LEVEL OF RISK

Natural course of elevated risk through the sales process.
Intended path of reduced risk through the sales process.

Marketing Campaign Objectives		
Objective 1	Objective 2	Objective 3
Build awareness, credibility, and trust with a prospect	*Facilitate the decision-making process*	*Lower the risk for your preferred prospect*
Tactics: Testimonials, referrals, and endorsements	Tactics: Differentiation and affirmation of value proposition	Tactics: Offensive and defensive strategies and/or positioning

loyal to a brand, service, or product simply by virtue that there isn't really any good reason not to.

Let's face it...we all like easy. We don't like to think too hard about every single decision we make in our day. Sometimes, we simply prefer to make choices on autopilot. While this facet doesn't tie directly to fear, it is connected. As I mentioned earlier, we fear the unknown. Because we fear the unknown, why would we spend time agonizing each time we are thirsty and want something to drink? If we know what we like, why not simply defer to those things we already know? For example, I consider myself "a Pepsi guy." My taste buds and palate simply prefer Pepsi products over Coke. Therefore, when I go grocery shopping or purchase a soda, given the option between Pepsi and nearly every other soda, I will choose Pepsi. Pepsi has become my default soda of choice and my buying habits reflect my preference despite attempts by Coke and others to lure me away through promotional sales, coupons, and so on. As long as Pepsi continues doing what it does, and I am not lured away by a newcomer to the game, I will remain a Pepsi guy.

However, pay close attention to that last sentence...: "As long as Pepsi continues to do what they do"—in other words, manufacture a tasty beverage and "I am not lured away by a newcomer." The consumer market is inundated with new products and services in hopes that companies can lure people away from a product offered by their competitors.

This concept goes back to the first goal of marketing, which is to create awareness, credibility, and trust. For example, let's say a new soda were to come out today and we will call it, "Best Soda Inc.". When first released, Best Soda Inc. will have zero brand awareness because until today, it never existed. It will have to go out and produce awareness so that people give it a try. If it is a good product, it will attract a following, and in time, people will likely begin to gravitate toward Best Soda. As more and more people like it, or key figures and celebrities jump on the bandwagon, a level of trust among consumers will be established. Now, Best Soda might not be everyone's favorite, and may not capture 100 percent of the soda market, but over time, it will likely attract more and more until it reaches a saturation point with its existing customer base. Over time, the company will have to continuously bring in and attract new people into its customer base to remain competitive.

But life is about perspective. As a consumer, consider the perspective of a company. It, too, is driven by experience and ultimately, fear. Every day, businesses fight in highly competitive markets. They are fighting for their survival. They are fighting to stay relevant and to be liked or preferred by consumers. They are fighting as organizations to maintain jobs and livelihood. They frame their image out of fear that if they don't produce products or services that satisfy consumers' needs and transform "wants" into needs, they will not survive.

The third purpose of marketing, according to Constantino is, "Lower the risk for your preferred prospect or customer to take the next step in the buying process." Immediately, one key word in that sentence should jump out at you—risk. Risk and fear are inextricably married to one another. We often fear risk because we cannot maintain certainty of a particular outcome. For a company, lowering risk means getting consumers to commit to buying the product or service, even before they have had an opportunity to try out alternatives. Lowering risk means giving consumers convincing reasons to choose the company's product or service. The company's message thus becomes, "We are saving you from wasting your time and money elsewhere because we are exactly what you need." Lowering risk also means offering money-back guarantees, good return policies, excellent customer service, and so on.

The next time you watch television, I encourage you to pay close attention to the commercials. How are companies trying to capture your business? How are they attempting to reach you, worry you, or assure you? When you watch commercials, start to take into consideration the pitches by industry and you will see that messages are often predictable. For example, a commercial for an insurance company will likely tell you how important it is, because when something bad happens, you will need them.

While scripts may vary from company to company, they essentially tell consumers the same thing, "We will be there for you when you need us. We are better than the other guy, and you and your family are too important to leave your insurance choice to chance...you need us."

Retailers attempt to reach consumers by telling them that if they want to "roll with the in-crowd," rather than being outcast or out of fashion, to shop their store. They have the hottest brands, best values, and what they offer is popular and socially acceptable. Some companies even pride themselves on their rebellious nature. "If you want to be different, and stand out, then pick us."

Consumer more likely to make the purchase.

Consumer less likely to make the purchase.

The reason that some marketing campaigns are more effective than others is, quite simply, they hit the right chord that resonates strongly with people at the right time. The more people who feel the message (that likely triggers fear in some form), the more impactful the marketing piece. This is precisely why marketing uses the same strategies...but different circumstances. People think with their heads, but they buy with their hearts. If your message, as a business, makes your consumers feel something, you are much more likely to attract them as customers than you would it you simply stated the facts.

What do they NEED that they don't have? How can YOUR product fill that need? As a company, in addition to a possible physical need, what emotional need does your product or service provide? How does your product make buyers feel? How and why does it do that? Can you convince them that they are better with your product than without it? These questions are essential when attempting to understand The METUS Principle and consumer economics.

Financial Market Trends

Financial markets are where companies, organizations, and even the government, go to raise needed capital Entities can sell stocks, bonds, and other financial instruments to the public to raise capital. Stocks, or shares, represent ownership in a company, while bonds represent borrowings on the part of a company, government entity, or other organization.

Investors, on the other side of the transaction, are looking for a place to purchase such vehicles to "park" their disposable funds and hopefully add to their investments through returns. These returns are expected to be sufficient to compensate for the risk of payment of interest and principle, as well as for the risk of default or failure.

There is an old Wall Street adage that markets move on fear and greed. It is worth noting that the notion of risk and fear go hand in hand. While bonds do carry some risk, which is usually denoted by the bond's rating (AAA to D ratings based on capacity to meet financial commitments, with AAA being the highest rating), bonds are generally considered safer investments than stocks. Stocks, while riskier, present an investor with a much greater opportunity for a sizeable return. As companies perform better, stock prices go up.

A more detailed discussion of financial markets would go beyond the scope of this book, which is based on a discussion of fear as motivation. That said, I would like to describe how investments and financial markets are built on and operate in a system driven by and manipulated by fear.

When talking finance and investing, there are two important terms that one must know. To be "bullish" means that an investor has a favorable outlook on the economy, and as a result, the market. If an investor is said to be "bearish," the investor lacks confidence in the economy and the market.

The actual origins of the terms "bear" and "bull" to describe market movements are unclear; the following is one of the more popular (from www.investopedia.com). The terms "bear" and "bull" are thought to derive from the way in which each animal attacks its opponents. That is, a bull will thrust its horns up into the air, while a bear will swipe down. These actions were then related metaphorically to the movement of a market: if the trend was up, it was considered a bull market; if the trend was down, it was a bear market.

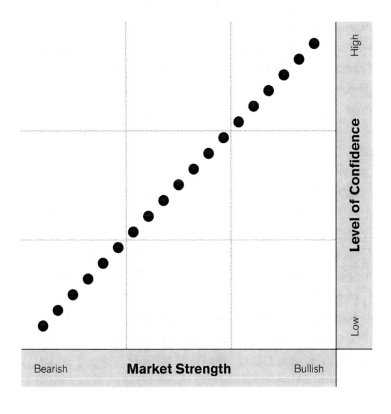

While many people may see themselves as knowledgeable or savvy investors, the truth is that only a small fraction of people truly have an expert degree of understanding when it comes to the economy. In fact, I will even go so far as to say many people who hold themselves out to be experts are nothing more than people who are parroting information they heard from someone else whom they hold in high regard and believe to be experts.

Even people who are *bona fide* experts are not always correct in predicting the market all the time. That is because situations and circumstances are always changing and each change produces a ripple effect in a society's buying habits. New products, new companies, and pop culture change daily, as do government policies and regulations. Even the actions of a single individual, depending on the action in question, can have a far-reaching impact on our markets.

Now let's consider the market from a bullish perspective. When stocks are trading higher, and a market is ascending, this is generally a result of certain factors. The demand for certain good and services is up, and performance indicators point to a willingness of consumers to spend their money. Typically, during a bullish economy, certain words are often associated with this type of market, such as "consumer confidence," "security," "prosperity," and "trust." In other words, bullish markets are created because society by and large is conducting its affairs with reduced fear, reduced anxiety, and a greater perception of certainty.

Conversely, let's look at the market from a bearish perspective. When stocks are down and the market is falling, this is also generally a result of certain factors. The demand for goods and services is down, performance indicators show that people are either opting to hold onto their money and/or they have less discretionary spending money available to them. Typically, during a bearish economy, words or phrases include "lack of consumer confidence," "anxiety," and "uncertainty." A bearish market is a reflection of how society feels about the environment. Pervasive fear will often lead to a recession, and even potentially a depression, if economic and societal fear grows strong enough.

There are all kinds of indicators or conditions that either reassure investors that our economy is moving in the right direction or that it is not. For the purpose of this book, I have elected not to go into great detail or specificity on what those are. Instead, the important take-away is that fear drives our economy and the markets provide us with a visible representation of how much fear there is or isn't throughout our society.

GOVERNMENT INVOLVEMENT
One of the most misunderstood factors related to the economy is government involvement. There are those who believe the economy would operate best with as little government involvement as possible. There are others who believe that government involvement is essential. Whatever camp you fall into, the bottom line is that both

the absence of government involvement and any degree of government involvement significantly impact a nation's economy.

The most basic question is: How does the government affect the economy? The short answer is through regulations, spending, policies, and conflict/war. The extent and manner to which it gets involved will most certainly have an effect on the economy. Why? Because each action or inaction produces a consequence.

In some cases, there are direct consequences. Direct consequences are the results that a regulation or policy is intended to have. The other outcome is an unintended consequence. An unintended consequence is a result that is related to, but not the intent of, a particular regulation or policy decision.

I will argue that the reason our nation's law books could fill huge libraries is that more than 90 percent of the laws on the books were created to address unintended consequences as a result of a particular regulation or policy decision that was enacted earlier.

For example, every regulation our government creates not only impacts a particular industry or sector of the economy, but also impacts many others. Consider the Environmental Protection Agency (EPA). The EPA was established by the federal government to protect human health and the environment by writing and enforcing regulations based on laws passed by Congress. The agency was created in the late 1950s and through the 1960s, by and large, it assumed an important role due to congressional reaction to increasing public concern about the impact human activity could have on the environment.

Specifically, the EPA was concerned about industrial pollution caused by industrial wastes and the burning of fossil fuels. At first glance, it is hard to argue with the purpose and goals of this particular agency. However, over time, the EPA has gained greater and greater authority, and as a result, many of its regulations and policies have had a damaging effect on our economy. Many industrial jobs have left our borders and moved overseas to nations with far fewer environmental regulations and barriers to production. As a result, many Americans have lost their jobs and jobs related to these particular industries have traveled with these companies overseas.

Furthermore, increased environmental regulations have led to a reduction in economic growth because it has gotten harder and harder to develop land and build buildings and facilities for commercial use. If you look at the skyline of the city of New York, much of what we see today, in terms of architecture, predates the EPA. Why? Because the EPA has made the building and development process so laborious, with so much red tape and added expenses, that many businesses opt not to build as long as they can.

In addition to government factors that are directly associated with reduced economic growth, there are also indirect factors that can be linked to government action. For example, the cost of construction. Some of you may be thinking, "Hey, wait, That's a free market!" Yes, and no. If and when government policies and union labor are involved, construction and labor costs rise quickly. So-called "green" initiatives can be—and often are—quite costly. It is therefore important to consider indirect, as well as more direct, factors that impact market conditions.

In some cases, the reward eventually outweighs the cost, and we do at times see expansion and growth. If you think I am wrong, take a moment to consider how much development occurred from 1850 to 1950 in America and how little has occurred since 1950 despite the fact that modern technology and equipment has developed exponentially during that time.

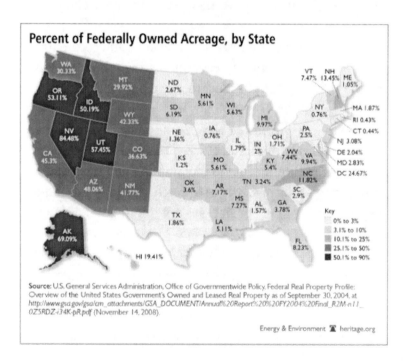

Percent of Federally Owned Acreage, by State

Source: U.S. General Services Administration, Office of Governmentwide Policy, Federal Real Property Profile: Overview of the United States Government's Owned and Leased Real Property as of September 30, 2004, at http://www.gsa.gov/gsa/cm_attachments/GSA_DOCUMENT/Annual%20Report%20%20FY2004%20Final_R2M-n11_0Z5RDZ-i34K-pR.pdf (November 14, 2008).

Energy & Environment heritage.org

Furthermore, look at how much development has occurred in China and how quickly they are able to erect an entire city in less time than it takes us to put up a single building in the United States. The reason isn't because of manpower or machinery—it is because of the extent of government involvement in each example.

Spending is another way in which the government can affect the economy. What is the government spending money on, how much, and why? Every day we hear reports regarding government spending. Surely we would not be bombarded by these reports if it weren't critical information. A government can spend money it doesn't have—this is known as "deficit spending." The government essentially spends money through borrowing with the expectation that it will capture that money at a later time through taxes. When economic conditions improve, more revenue is collected by the Treasury because there is more money circulating in the economy. At other times, the government levies additional taxes to justify and cover additional spending. Either way, these decisions impact the economy.

Military conflict is another vehicle through which the decisions of the government affect the economy. Decisions to intervene or abstain from conflict are more important today than ever because we operate in a global economy. Turmoil in the Middle East not only affects people in the Middle East, but that turmoil can result in higher oil prices, energy costs, manufacturing costs, and so on. The question really becomes: How much control does government have over state, federal, or international economies? In my opinion, based on the METUS Principle, government has a lot of control.

The single-most important responsibility our government has is to ensure the protection and security of its people. This protection extends not only to a person in the physical sense, but also to a person's property. Again, consider Maslow's hierarchy and the progression from basic needs to more advanced needs. The obligation and responsibility of government should be, first and foremost, to mitigate fear by ensuring law and order (safety need on Maslow's hierarchy). This law and order should extend only to the protection of one man over another, and not protect a man from himself, which were exactly the intentions of our Founding Fathers. However, more than ever, our government has extended its reach well beyond its intended reach, and now has a greater control over our economy than at any other time in history.

Thomas Paine, in his essay, *The Rights of Man*, suggested, at least in part, that a government may in fact be the single largest manipulator of economics by virtue of regulatory authority, discretionary spending authority, taxing authority, and its ability to engage in mass conflict.

Starting with the idea of war, Paine did not care for war. He lamented that a quarter or more of a worker's income was absorbed by taxes, perceiving a direct link between high taxes and war. War, through increased tax revenue, grows government, or other words, Paine believed that "takings" were the art of conquering at home. According to Paine, "Taxes are not raised to carry on war, but that war is raised to carry on taxes."

It is my belief, through the lens of the METUS Principle, that this is true not only of actual warfare, but of "manufactured" warfare as well. Motives speak to citizen fears to justify the means—that is, raising taxes to increase government presence. Greater government presence increases government power, which is why governments have little incentive to work toward perpetual peace.

Simply said, governments have a vested interest in war because it can use fear to justify the ends; both personal and public. The people of any nation engaged in war are harmed by it either physically, psychologically, monetarily, economically, or all the above.

It is my belief that we are witnessing Paine's fear and sentiment, and that as a nation, we have been living under the umbrella of Paine's fear in earnest since World War I, aside from a brief bout of isolationism before entering the second World War. Since WWII, the U.S. has been consistently engaged in some conflict or another, including the Cold War, Korean War, Vietnam War, Gulf War, and the "War on Terror," just to name a few.

The fact is that the U.S. has historically found itself in a perpetual state of warfare, and when you consider our involvement within the context of Paine's view on war, it is hard to argue that our constant involvement in international conflict hasn't been a justification for increased taxation, which has resulted in a gradual increase in burden on the American people. Our constant involvement in various conflicts has had economic implications for our nation; these wars have been the justification of countless policies and regulations that have been thrust upon the American people by its government.

I will even go so far as to argue that the "War on Poverty," the "War on Global Warming," the "War on Obesity," the "War on Women," and so on, are all manufactured conflicts to justify spending and raising taxes. All of these "wars" have had substantial consequences to the American economy either directly, indirectly, or both.

If you consider how many trillions of dollars have been levied to fight these manufactured wars, and that the citizenry has really not seen any significant return on its investments, again it becomes hard to argue with Paine's assertion that wars are used to justify taxation and that such taxation is a means of passive oppression by government.

SUMMARY

From the perspective of the METUS Principle, the idea of war can evoke both potential and actual fear. People actually fear war because of the pain and suffering it causes. News reports broadcast he destruction and devastation, as well as the loss of lives. For those fighting or those who have loved ones in the active military, this fear is especially powerful.

People potentially fear war because of the uncertainty that surrounds it. Who will be affected by war or conflict? Will the war gain momentum, spread or cause adverse chain reactions?

Looking at Maslow's hierarchy, one could argue that manipulating war can impact all five levels in some capacity, especially the psychological needs and those of safety and security.

As long as government manipulates fear, both actually and potentially, government can subsequently interfere with citizens' ability to progress toward a state of self-actualization, if and when it deems this appropriate. Through such interference, government is able to retain importance in peoples' lives by making itself needed. Rather than being self-reliant, people opt to turn to government to fulfill their needs and solve their problems.

If people are able to achieve the more progressive states of Maslow's hierarchy, government would cease to exist—it would no longer be valued by the general populous. If government were no longer valued, people would no longer willingly give up a significant proportion of their income to keep it running.

Given that the government has incentive to induce fear, and the general populous is both susceptible and has limited ability to recognize, manage, and mitigate such fear, the average citizen finds himself or herself caught in a perpetual cycle that is favorable to government and influential elite who have the resources to mitigate the fears the average citizen cannot.

Government controls the flow of money. It can cut or raise the amount of funds made available for social programs, infrastructure repairs, and so much more. In addition, the government plays a huge role in our economy. As long as government stands to benefit from the manufacture of fear, it will continue to manipulate and perpetuate those fears.

NOTES

CHAPTER SEVEN
POLITICS AND FEAR

Evan Wynn's Story:

[Retired] State Legislator and United States Military Veteran

At the heart of leadership is a servant's mentality. True leaders are always looking out for others – to make the lives of others better. Evan Wynn is a great example of a person who has dedicated his life to the service of others. In 1980, Evan enlisted in the United States Marine Corps Reserves; In 1986, he made the decision to serve his country full-time and he enlisted in the United States Army, where he served for twenty years, completing his duties in 2006 with a final rank of Master Sergeant. In 2010, Wynn became a state representative in the Wisconsin State Assembly, serving the citizens of the 43rd District.

An Iraqi war veteran, Wynn was awarded a number of service honors, which include the Legion of Merit, Bronze Star, Meritorious Service Medal (3 times), Army Commendation Medal (5 times), Army Achievement Medal (9 times), U.S. Army and Australian Parachutist Wings, and the Air Assault Badge. While in the Army, Wynn made the decision to volunteer for paratrooper duties and would eventually be assigned to the 82nd Airborne Division and 325th Airborne Infantry Regiment.

When I hear the words, "paratrooper" and
"skydiving," the first thing that pops into my head is a
phrase I once recall reading in *Band of Brothers* and a
variation of the quote often referred to in today's pop
culture; "[Why would anyone want] to jump out of a
perfectly good airplane." For many people, this is
certainly a reasonable question. For others, jumping out
of an airplane may appear second nature. What I would
eventually learn is that jumping out of an airplane was not
second nature for Evan; and in fact, Evan is afraid of
heights. That's right; I did not say *was* afraid of heights...I
said that he IS afraid of heights.

When I first learned that Evan is afraid of heights,
and was a paratrooper and Master Sergeant, I was
immediately intrigued. I wanted to learn more about why
someone who is afraid of heights would voluntarily take
on a position as a paratrooper. When I asked Evan about
his motivation, he first referred to a song he remembered
from his childhood. It was a song from 1968 entitled, *The
Green Berets*. The song referred to "wings upon my chest
to show the world I was America's best." For Wynn, it
wasn't enough to just be a part of military and serve his
country – he also wanted to be one of America's best. "I
realized that I would have to overcome my fear if I
wanted to become a paratrooper. All through Airborne
School, I kept a set of wings in my locker. I kept my mind
focused on the goal instead of my fear. However, I knew
later that I never overcame my fear of heights – I still have

it to this day – I just managed my fear by staying focused on my duty. Throughout the rest of my career, I kept my mind focused on my mission, prayed, and left the rest to the Lord."

During my conversations with Evan, I also remembered a time he shared with me; he was aboard a plane and preparing to make a training jump on Fort Bragg's Sicily Drop Zone. "As we were getting near the drop zone, we started our pre-jump procedures, which included checking our equipment. This is when I noticed that my static line safety pin and lanyard were missing from my static line snap hook." Wynn said. Of course, when you are jumping out of an airplane with nothing but a parachute on your back to keep you safe, you want to make entirely certain that your equipment is in proper working order.

The static line safety pin is used to make sure the snap hook does not open. If it opens and falls off the static line, your main parachute will not open. "I could have been pulled from the jump due to this missing piece of equipment. My soldiers were behind me. I knew that I had a reserve in case my main parachute did not open," he said.

On the one hand, I understand Wynn's logic. He didn't know for certain that his main chute would not open properly, and even if it didn't, that is what the reserve chute is for. On the other hand, it is also reasonable to assume that if the main chute was potentially defective, and missing key pieces, that other important pieces may be missing as well – including pieces in his reserve chute. But these were not thoughts that came to Wynn. Instead, Evan immediately thought about his men. "I was a Staff Sergeant. I was a leader. I had to ignore the fear and make the jump with my soldiers." He said. "I went through the procedure on how to deploy my reserve in my mind and said a quick prayer."

It wasn't that Evan didn't consider the potential consequences of what he was about to do – he did. However, those consequences were more personal in nature. He carefully considered the risks of jumping, and the risks of not jumping. Yes, there were risks if he chose not to jump. At that moment, Wynn recognized that he was a leader. All of the other soldiers aboard that plane were privates and specialists (E1-E4). Because of the great leaders he had around him and from whom he had learned from over the years, he understood the importance of putting the needs of his men before his own. They needed reassurance that everything would be okay, and they looked to their leader for reassurance. Now, aboard the plane, Wynn was that leader, just as many of his mentors were to him earlier in his career. He knew that if their Squad Leader did not make the jump, the decision could have negative implications during situations beyond training. He could not show fear. "I know that by going through the jump, their fears and anxiety would not be raised," said Wynn.

* * * * *

Most people do not really want freedom,
because freedom involves responsibility,
and most people are frightened of responsibility.
—Sigmund Freud

The political machine triumphs because it is united minority
acting against a divided majority.
—Will Durant

I am drawn to the words of President John F. Kennedy in his 1961 presidential inaugural address, "Ask not what your country can do for you, ask what you can do for your country," and have come to reflect and understand that statement in a broader sense. This simple statement asked people to look toward a cause beyond himself or herself and work hard for the greater good of the nation. A clarifying accompaniment of JFK's statement could read, "Ask not what your country or countrymen can do for you, but ask what you can do for yourself."

Politics (from Greek *politicos),* is defined as, "of, for, or relating to citizens." Its perspective can take on both an art or science context when describing how politicians go about influencing people on a civic or individual level. Modern political discourse often focuses on democracy and the relationship between people and politics. It is thought of as the way we "choose" government officials and make decisions about public policy. However, from the perspective of the METUS Principle, to truly understand politics, it is less important to focus on society or the masses, but rather, to focus on the individual.

Once you understand how a person thinks and his or her motivation, it is much easier to develop strategies that guide the person's decision. As a politician, or any leader for that matter, you cannot successfully lead a million people if you cannot lead one. Because the METUS Principle addresses the lowest common denominator with respect to human motivation and decision-making— fear—the concept can be used to successfully impact one or many people. In other words, concepts are transferable.

If we are to believe that any society is only as strong as its weakest link, would it not make sense for us to encourage one another to be our very best and to expect that same effort of ourselves? While there are certainly some people with physical, emotional, or cognitive limitations, should those limitations excuse a person from giving his or her best effort?

The answer is no. A person will often live up to, or down to, expectations. So why not encourage, motivate, and support each other in setting the bar high and working hard toward individual goals? Even if we are not able to attain our ultimate goals, our society as a whole will certainly be better off when each person's best effort is directed at improving his or her situation.

If society were to develop in such a way that required or encouraged individuals to give their best effort, we might better understand and realize the words of JFK. It may seem rather ironic to some that by serving ourselves, we can better serve our country and our fellow man.

The single sentence spoken by JFK—"Ask not what your country can do for you, but what you can do for your country"—has served as a catalyst for discussion that goes beyond merely scratching the surface of partisan debate. It speaks to the heart of politics, which at its core, is truly about each single, solitary voter. A candidate may be an extraordinary person, but if he or she cannot develop a strategy to reach citizens (constituents), that candidate is no good to anyone, politically speaking.

Politics has many fine lines and gray areas. Politicians routinely struggle between doing what is, or what they perceive to be, right—and doing what is in their best interest politically. Over time, politicians work on amassing "good will" with the public. This is sometimes referred to as "political capital." Of course, the easiest way for politicians to remain in good favor with people is to give them everything they want. However, doing so—keeping everyone happy all the time—is virtually impossible.

The government itself owns nothing; what it has is the responsibility to oversee the use of collected public resources (taxes) to benefit the public at large. Any time the government "gives" something away, or develops policies that are favorable to some people, it is doing so at the expense of others. Anything the government bestows is first taken away from before it is given to. In some cases, what is taken is given back in the form of services or goods, and while what is taken may not be returned in a proportional manner, there are many examples in which the public is more or less content. Various historical figures, such as John Locke, Thomas Hobbes, and Jean-

Jacques Rousseau, have written very good pieces on social contract theory, but again, they tend to focus on society at large as opposed to focusing on individuals.

Founding Father James Madison recognized all too well that democracy has a fatal flaw. As he worked with his brethren to craft America's new system of government, the Founders tried to safeguard against any possibilities of the citizens using the system to vote themselves a living. Yet, despite their foresight and best efforts, many policies have been created along the lines of *quid pro quo* arrangements, in which politicians agree to support policies that reward a segment of the population at the expense of another. In doing so, the segment of citizens that is rewarded subsequently votes for those who bestowed favors upon them.

In a democracy, the takers can overwhelm the makers. Once the people realize they can vote themselves a comfortable life, rather than work for one, it is very hard for a democracy to survive.

It is human nature to look for the path of least resistance. Many people would rather look to government to provide for their welfare, rather than relying on themselves and their own effort. Plain and simple...it is easier.

Others would rather rely on themselves than relying on social welfare systems, even though it is harder. They are willing to look the possibility of failure right in the eye and say, "Bring it on!" They are willing to put in the time and to believe in themselves and their efforts. Yet, despite their boldness and desire to succeed, many fail. Some even fail countless times. However, these driven people don't give up, they don't quit on themselves, and they do not look to others to bail them out. They keep working. They persevere through adversity. They continue to recognize the chance of failure, but they endure and continue working to make something of themselves. Until the late 20th century and continuing on into the 21st century, creating one's own success was the American Dream—a dream upon which the United States was founded.

So the question becomes, "Why do some people continue to persevere and work hard when it is easier not to?" The answer can be found using the METUS Principle. All of us are pre-programmed to fear. It is nature and each of our individual experiences that impact what exactly it is that we are afraid of. While fear is static, and does not change, what we are afraid of is dynamic and does change over time, sometimes significantly. Every one of us makes choices based on actual fear (concrete threats to our survival) and potential fear (fears over which we have no control or are solely in our minds). Our decisions are based on what we are more afraid of, that which is (actual) or that which could be (potential).

When people quit or give up, they are giving into their actual fear. Actual fear may be described using terms as, "No matter how hard I try, I will never be able to do it" or "I'm just not good enough." People who choose to quit are afraid that no matter how hard they work, they will never accomplish their goal or something they desire. In fact, they may even fear the hard work itself—emphasis on the word *hard*. Carol Dwerk, a professor at Stanford University, refers to this mindset as "fixed versus growth."

According to Dwerk, through more than three decades of systematic research, she has been attempting to answer the question as to why some people achieve their potential while equally talented others don't? Why some even appear to exceed their potential, while others do not even come close to realizing theirs. The key, she found, isn't ability; it's whether you look at ability as something inherent that needs to be demonstrated or as something that can be developed. Those who have a "fixed mindset" believe that "[things] are the way they are," but that doesn't mean that they have less of a desire for a positive self-image than anyone else. So of course they want to perform well and look smart; however, they fail to take the necessary personal steps that are needed to achieve what they desire. They view success as a challenge and fear the realization that success is not assured even if you work hard. Rather than risk failing and negatively impacting their self-image, they will often avoid challenges and stick to what they know they can do well.

> *Don't blame Caesar, blame the people of Rome who have rejoiced in their loss of freedom, who hail him when he speaks in the Forum of more security, more living fatly at the expense of the industrious.*
> —Marcus Cicero

People who hold the "growth mindset" believe that intelligence can be developed, that the brain is like a muscle that can be trained. This leads to the desire to improve. Growth minded people embrace challenges, because they know that they will emerge stronger by putting in time and effort toward achieving their desired goals.

In Dwerk's research, she has been able to identify a mindset; one that recognizes, understands, and manages fear in order to achieve their goals and an alternative mindset of people who are limited by their inability to do so.

Dwerk's research is compelling for a variety of reasons, mainly, because she concludes that a person is able to change his or her way of thinking from a fixed mindset to a growth mindset under the right conditions. With this understanding, the best approach to social policy is creating policies that encourage and help people to develop a growth mindset as well as promoting hard work, effort, perseverance, and determination, as opposed to those that encourage people to quit on themselves.

In my view, there is a simple reason we have competing views in society. The reason is that fear is extremely powerful and many politicians have learned that they can manipulate the fears of others for their own advantage. Some politicians support policies of dependence so that they are needed, and when they are needed, they maintain their power base. If people did not need them, or perceived the politicians had nothing to offer them, other politicians would swoop in and attempt to fill that void.

As a result, politics is a vicious cycle or manipulating and in some cases, actually manufacturing fear.

A great society is one that focuses on creating policies that promote a hand up, not one that encourages hand-outs. A social safety net should limit failure, rather than promote mediocrity and simplicity. With respect to Maslow's hierarchy of needs, a government can address only the bottom rung of Maslow's hierarchy—safety, shelter, sustenance—and subsequently, can keep people living in a state of perpetual fear. When people look to the government, society, or others to meet their needs, they will always live in fear. If people routinely rely on others, those others have the ability to take away what is given at any time. Conversely, if they rely on themselves and their individual efforts, they will feel empowered. Empowered people fear less because they believe they have greater control over their destiny .

Because sound concepts should transcend time and place, I initially intended to discuss fear within existing political theories. However, I believe it would be easier to consider the METUS Principle using tangible examples.

WHAT DOES POLITICAL FEAR LOOK LIKE?
Politicians throughout history, and particularly in the 21st century, have used fear as a way to influence voters, and voter preferences. In recent times, we have witnessed politicians able to present themselves as the antithesis of fear, in favor of promoting prosperity for all. A prosper-ous, cared for nation, and a better way of leading the nation are appealing statements to citizens that have

expressed concern that the system was broken and that politicians had taken advantage of their positions for personal gain for far too many years. People want better, and when a promise of better presents itself, voters were given every reason to believe that the next politics, and the country, could be different than what people had come to expect from their government in years past.

Conversely, many politicians attempted to project fear, and cast doubt upon their opposition. With a struggling economy, real or perceived continuation back-office political deals, and a very divisive political land-scape across the nation, using fear against one's opponent also proved a successful and useful tool for politicians. By casting doubt, and attempting to project fear, both incumbents and challengers across the country attempted to argue that a government led by one's opponent was a dangerous proposition.

Fear-mongering, using strawmen, scapegoating, demagoging, and demonizing are all strategies used to manipulate people through fear. These methods speak directly to people's insecurities, self-doubts, and the threats to basic human needs. The political system uses fear, and perpetuates fear, in order to achieve both personal and party goals. Politics is a system designed to operate from one crisis to another eliciting fears that influence policy.

As experts develop more sophisticated research methods, and gain a more accurate understanding of what causes people to act, advisors on both sides of the political aisle further advance the use of fear in influencing voters. Twenty-first century politics has not only attempted to manipulate the fears of voters, but in many cases have boldly developed strategies to manufacture fear. Through threats of sequestration, economic uncertainty, and looming international threats, politicians have aimed to project possible catastrophes upon one another, while simultaneously working toward distancing themselves from any potential negative outcomes associated with these crises.

This strategic and multidimensional use of fear is rather remarkable. In fact, in March of 2013, nearly every poll taken indicated that the majority of Americans disapproved of the direction the country was headed. However, polls also suggest that people are unsure on where to place blame. In many instances voters supported current policy decisions, but disliked the results of the policy. What this tells us is that the multidimensional aspect, in which fear was cast, made it very difficult for the average person to determine who was at fault for the problems that were clearly rampant across the country.

In other words, politicians were successfully able to simultaneously project fear and deflect it. Across the country citizens were hearing speeches, or in most cases sound bites, in which an elected representative would portray him or herself as a fighter, fighting for them, the average American. They would eloquently express their displeasure for current problems facing our nation, and make sure their audience was aware that they were vigilant—fighting against those who want to inflict pain, inflict misery, and those who have caused the citizens pain and misery. In these speeches they would lobby for their policies, inciting that if voters did not band together and adopt their policies, things were sure to get far worse.

How can this possibly work? The strategy requires a strategic two-front approach, which has required elected officials to deflect fear away from him or herself and project fear on those in which they seek to blame. Using the METUS Principle, a politician is able to manipulate actual fear, which is what Americans face in their present sense, on those that oppose their own vague policy and agenda. The average American links their message of fighting for the citizen, and for the country, to his or her policy, which successfully deflects any causes of fear away from themselves. In those same speeches, they simultaneously project fear onto others; their political opponents. Whoever communicates their message better, or is more convincing, generally wins the argument regardless of which policy position is actually better, or in some cases, whom is actually to blame for poor economic conditions. Speeches that are both reassuring and condemning can go a long way in winning the hearts and minds of the average voter.

There is another angle in manipulating fear, and that angle is in reference to potential fear. By demanding policies that go far beyond any reasonable compromise, in which bipartisan support may alleviate such a hostile and contentious political environment, politicians have instead preferred using fear throughout the legislative process. Depending on which party controls the executive branch and the legislative branch in a given state, or which party controls the executive branch and the legislative branch at the Federal level, opposing parties have attempted to make demands of one another knowing that their demand(s) will not be agreed upon. What we eventually get is some level of compromise in order to get something passed and signed into law.

In most cases, the party with more bargaining chips will get most of what it is asking for, and if or when conditions do not improve, they argue to voters that it is because many provisions in the proposed bill were blocked in favor of a modified bill. Each side then takes turns blaming one another for the failing outcomes and argue that the bill did not accomplish what their version of their bill was intended to do. Opposing parties will then make new demands on one another and the cycle begins again. Politicians that have been able to manipulate both short-term and long-term fear, and position him or herself as a fighter against pain and misery, have faired far better and have allowed them to maintain their positions of power.

In fairness to our 21st-century politicians, the use of fear to influence the masses goes back centuries before them. As long as their has been organized government, with some leading the many, fear has been used in some capacity. To some degree, every politician uses fear; both actual and implied. From the minute a politician enters a race for office, he or she develops a strategy for winning the race or the election. Strategies center around "needs," and needs can be linked straight to Abraham Maslow. A politician must determine what exactly his or her voting base wants and how he or she can deliver.

Let us for a minute look at the system from a slightly different perspective. I will ask you, "Is it what each candidate purports to give, or is it what they are eliminating that wins elections?" For example, let's use social welfare. In some voting districts, creating additional social welfare programs is a winning message, while in other districts, it would be a loser. How can this be? If it were simply the "giving away" aspect that was a winner, than surely social welfare programs should be popular everywhere.

To understand why some districts are for and why some districts are against creating additional social welfare programs, consider the METUS Principle. Central to the METUS Principle is a pyramid, which represents Maslow's hierarchy of needs. As a general rule, communities with very low socioeconomic status have greater needs related to those referred to as basic, found at the bottom or base of the pyramid. In higher socioeconomic communities, as a general rule, families do not typically struggle to meet basic needs. Politicians who promote higher taxes and favor social welfare programs, gain favor with those who do not have their basic needs met.

For starters, the poor in America pay very few taxes, regardless of their respective geographic location. There are both federal and state policies that operate on a graduated income system of taxation, and as a result, those who earn very little are allowed to keep most of their income, and in some cases, all of what they make. Furthermore, the tax code also allows some families to get back more than they contribute—this is social welfare. In communities in which a person earns very little and has very little, there is little concern with tax rates (what is taken) versus what is given (social welfare). As a result, people in lower socio-economic status (SES) communities favor voting for candidates who are likely to give the most, as opposed to those who are willing to take the least.

Now, contemplate those who are considered wealthy. People who are rich rarely have to worry about basic needs—food, water, shelter, and so on. Nor are they overly concerned with taxes, because despite what is taken, they know they will still have more than enough. Depending on their level of wealth, since they are not concerned about gaining from the system, nor are they overly concerned with what is taken, they are often motivated by what they see as their social duty or responsibility, a responsibility to give back to those less fortunate.

In many affluent communities, people are often "guilted" into maintaining a certain political view and voting a certain way. Those at the top of the elite power base will ostracize people in their communities to fall in line, and in some cases, make the lives of others difficult so that they conform.

In various discussions across the country, I have often pointed to Hollywood to illustrate this point. For many wealthy Americans, their environment drives their fear. "What will people think?" and "How will my choices affect my career?" For those wielding power and manipulating such fear, it is another way for them to maintain their own power base.

These voting examples are, and they may seem, a generalization. Not all poor Americans will vote in favor of social welfare, not all middle class Americans will vote for lower taxes, and not all wealthy Americans will defer to an established power base. There are, of course, other environmental factors that will influence such decisions.

It is important to keep in mind, however, that even though there are other variables and circumstances, they are all rooted in fear and can be explained by the METUS Principle. A person's past experiences, current state, and vision for the future will all impact the decisions a person makes and are all influenced by a real or perceived fear that serves as a catalyst for decisions that are made.

I believe that people who best exploit fear-based methods for personal or professional gain are in fact fearful people. They recognize fear in themselves and use this fear to their own personal advantage. Those who have channeled their fear in more productive ways, and have found peace within their own efforts, often have a far more difficult time reaching the masses in a manner that speaks to peoples' emotions. They tend to present themselves in a more logical manner because that is the lens through which they see the world. Those who have learned to manage or control their own fear, who try to use emotion and fear to motivate others to act, often tend to come across as unauthentic, fake, or disingenuous. They are trying to be something they are not.

In politics today, there is a lot of talk about political messaging. The question for those running for political office becomes, "How do I engage a disinterested voter just enough to get the person to vote?" Achieving this goal requires a very simple message that is not only easy to understand, but resonates in a way that requires some action. A message may be simple and easy to understand, but it doesn't necessarily elicit an action response. So, what is the difference between a simple message that inspires people to act and one that does not? A message that is simple and effective must speak to a person's emotions. According to the METUS Principle, a person is most likely to act when the emotion involved is fear, because fear triggers the survival instinct.

It is much easier to influence disengaged voters through their emotions than through logic, because emotion allows a candidate to speak to them in short, concise sound bytes. When people hear something that makes them feel a certain way, that message has been successful. Another reason that tugging on the emotions of voters is effective in drawing votes is because it does not require an audience to understand science, reason, facts, and perhaps most importantly, the context of the information being presented. In some cases, simple messages aimed at eliciting an emotional response may claim statistics as fact, but can usually be proven wrong when applying true scientific reasoning or even general logic.

To the engaged and informed mind, arguments based entirely on emotion usually fail to hold water. Those with disengaged minds or who remain uninformed are content to block out the facts and allowing emotion to guide their thinking (and voting).

As kids, we dream about what we will be. However, sometimes fear gets between that dream and our reality. We hit a point at which we fail to give our best, and may recognize that it is easier not to strive or struggle to achieve our goals, or to be satisfied with mediocrity. Some people will then look to others for support. Some will even look to government, because let's face it...it is easier to rely on others rather than picking ourselves up, dusting ourselves off, and trying again. In doing so, they become accustomed to relying on others rather than relying on themselves.

In my opinion, success is freedom and freedom is success. Conversely, captivity is failure and failure is captivity. Once we put our fate and livelihood in the hands of others, rather than creating our own destiny, we have become captive.

CAN THE METUS PRINCIPLE OF FEAR BE USED TO EXPLAIN DEMOCRACY ?

Perhaps one of the greatest American philosophers was John Dewey (1859-1952). From a public policy perspective, Dewey strongly believed that philosophy must inquire into the real needs of democracy in America. It must provide a means to address society's social problems, tendencies, work forces, and possibilities for improvement.

Dewey's work emphasizes that a society that does not promote maximizing individual potential will become stagnant at best, but more likely will decay from the establishment of unsustainable free-rider-type conditions. Furthermore, a society that promotes collectivism at the expense of individualism creates less prosperity for everyone, as unrealized human potential not only hurts the individual, but also society at large.

Dewey wasn't alone in his reverence for individual self-determinism. Founding Fathers John Locke, Thomas Jefferson, and Adam Smith were also committed to the innate individuality of all people. These are best described as self-evident, inalienable rights, the very rights upon which the United States was founded: life, liberty, and the pursuit of happiness. In all practicality, a collectivist approach does nothing more than allow a small few to prosper at the expense of the majority.

Our nation is still, at least for the time being, living off the deterministic prosperity of previous generations, while at the same time, borrowing against the prosperity of future generations. This failure to make our own way can be seen through a lens of insecurity, which Dewey calls "the child of scarcity." He believed that he was living in an era marked by economic insecurity, political apathy, and deep decline of religion and family. This pattern has accelerated from Dewey's generation into present day. Larger societal problems are a result of unthinking conformity, crime, and the general disregard for other people; , which, at the most fundamental level, are a result of mismanaged fear.

In the United States, political leaders have been too concerned with legislating prosperity and not concerned enough with developing a strong, confident, capable work force that would take care of those problems through individual effort. Government doesn't create prosperity; individuals do. For a society to prosper, individuals need to succeed; a group cannot succeed without the effort of individuals. Since the government is nothing more than a large, collective representation of a group—the American people—so too is it impossible for the government to create success. The more individuals who work hard and succeed, the more successful a society will be. However, those who rely on others to provide them with a living may see this concept as completely foreign.

There is nothing more unequal than the equal treatment of unequal people.
—Thomas Jefferson

Consider a basic illustration to demonstrate my point. There are two businesses: Business #1 and Business #2. Both employ six people. All six employees at Business #1 work hard, meet performance goals, and share in the daily profits. Business #2 also has six employees. Three work hard and meet or exceed performance goals, the other three perform at a mediocre level, and still share equally in the daily profits.

Which business and group of six employees do you expect will earn more, accomplish more, and perform better? Members of Business #1 may have experienced higher earnings on some days than others, but over time, all employees contribute at a level consistent with their counterparts, while in Business #2, only half of the group contributes toward the good of the whole. This illustration demonstrates the difference between individualism and collectivism.

How long do you think the three hard-working employees in Business #2 will keep striving and allow the other three to free ride? One of two primary outcomes will occur: the three committed workers will choose not to work as hard because they are not able to realize the true benefits of their work or they may decide to split off from the mediocre workers because they see no advantage to remaining partners with the three others who do not contribute to their outcome.

A collectivist approach can only last as long as the productive members of a group continue to give the free riders a free pass, which is a major reason there is a predictable cycle of democracy .

From a political perspective, this concept can be illustrated perfectly using Alexander Tytler's "Cycle of Democracy." Tytler's model itself suggests that the life cycle of a democracy is about 200 years and progresses through nine distinct phases. The reason democracy is a cycle is because motivation, which I contend is based on fear, will elicit slightly different response actions by the majority, as well as those in positions of leadership, depending on which particular phase a society finds itself.

In some phases, actual fear is greater than potential fear; and in other phases, potential fear is greater than actual fear. It is fear that motivates action. Based on Tytler's model, fear motivation can be predictive, and thus, it creates a cycle.

The origin of a democracy grows out of bondage as it transitions to spiritual faith. A person in bondage knows no freedom because he or she exists for the primary reason to serve another. A person in bondage fears

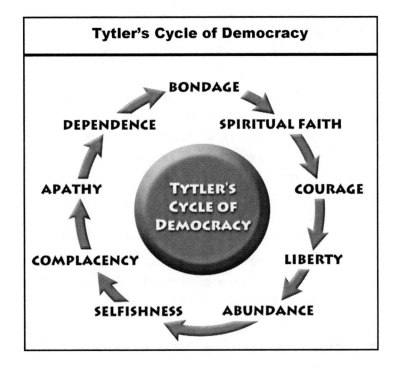

captivity and the absence of individual liberty, but with no means to escape, finds comfort in a deepening appreciation of spiritual faith.

Faith gives people hope and guides them and within certain passages they are made to feel strong. Although they may have limited means, in the actual sense, people who have faith believe that they may become more, potentially. What a person lacks, in the actual sense, and what a person may become, in the potential sense, is a very powerful and motivating force. If a person has nothing to lose, but much to again, this sense manifests itself in courage.

A courageous person is not someone who lives with limited or well-managed fear. Instead, a person who is courageous fears his or her actual state and believes that the potential to improve is worth the risk. In other words, a person who has limited means and absence of freedom, is more afraid of continuing to live the life he or she is living than fearing death in search of liberty.

From liberty comes abundance. When a person has a great work ethic, is empowered, and is liberated, he or she goes in search of excellence. Such people embrace a hearty individualism and seek to make something of themselves. In doing so, they reap the fruits of their labor, which results in a surplus of prosperity, or abundance. The phase of democracy between liberty and abundance is the closest a society can come to a collective degree of self -actualization. Although examples can be offered both historically and globally, particularly in small tribal settings, it is my assertion based on centuries of documented evidence as well as examples from present day, that the human species is not well designed for collectivist living; and as a result, abundance eventually shifts to selfishness.

Selfishness occurs when people compare their happiness and satisfaction against that of others. It involves the principle of coveting a neighbor's belongings rather than being happy with what one has and what one has worked for. Those who are selfish are less concerned about having what they need, but rather, having what they want and what others have. A selfish person is "out to get his," which more often is achieved at the expense of others.

From selfishness develops complacency. A person who is complacent isn't necessarily concerned with working hard; instead, he or she is simply pleased with having "his or hers." This is a smug, self-righteous existence that accelerates decay. A person who is complacent fears what is potential, rather than what is actual. What is actual is comfortable, and requires very little effort; what is potential requires work. Complacent people fears the hard work that would be required to reach their potential. This could also be described just as easily as a blue-blood, trust-fund mentality.

From a societal complacency comes apathy. To a casual observer, complacency and apathy may appear as one and the same. However, they are distinctly different in one key manner: Complacency is the subtle, conscious decision to accept what one has rather than go out with the desire to accomplish more. Apathy, on the other hand, is learned from others, mainly from the preceding generation. An apathetic generation watched its parents and others coast through life and were not taught the values of hard work or self-determinism. An apathetic generation was taught, in many cases unwittingly, to avoid hard work and look for the path of least resistance.

From a generation of apathy a generation of dependency is created. Essentially, no money or resources remain from the age of abundance. The generations of complacency and apathy have drained the piggy banks and used all resources left to them for their own self-serving ends. They did not contribute to societal improvement much at all, and as a result, many of their children will pay the price. As a result, fear has transitioned from a greater state of potentiality to a greater state of actuality. Members of a dependent society have nothing unless something is given to them by others. Dependent people fear for their everyday survival, and as a result, think very little about their potential. Every day is a day they try to find just enough to get by.

A dependent society is one that, in a short time, will once again find itself in bondage. Over time, there will simply not be enough resources to go around. People will turn to anyone who claims to provide them with a better life and addresses their needs. From their innate fear for survival will arise someone who promises to be a provider, who will gain power through promises he or she cannot possibly keep. This person will exploit the fears of those who depend on the promise the most, and in the end, will deliver them back into bondage. Once people return to a state of bondage, the cycle can begin anew.

WHY ARE SOCIALISM, COMMUNISM, AND UNIONISM SO APPEALING?

The draw of socialism, communism, and unionism is grounded in the idea of fairness, and in some cases, protection. Socialism can be defined as any of various theories or systems of social organization in which the means of producing and distributing goods is owned collectively or by a centralized government that often plans and controls the economy.

Communism is a theoretical economic system characterized by the collective ownership of property and by the organization of labor for the common advantage of all members.

Unionism is a combination of people so formed, especially an alliance or confederation of workers, parties, or political entities, for mutual interest or benefit.

These "-isms" have one distinct feature in common: the public ownership of one another's success and one another's failure. Socialists, communists, and union members look to each other to ensure their livelihood. Their leaders promise fairness, equality, and protection to their followers. They promise to prevent failure rather than promoting individual prosperity.

Labor unions focus heavily on negotiating working conditions, pay, benefits, and disciplinary actions for their members. In many cases, unions value seniority (the length of time someone has been at a job) over productivity (how good one is at his or her job). A union mentality, at its very core, centers on the protection of its members.

Consider this; if you worked hard to be the best you could be, at whatever it was you wanted to be the best, wouldn't you want to be rewarded on the basis of your effort, as opposed to the efforts of those around you? If you were the best, wouldn't you want to work for an employer who rewarded your skills, your talents, and your ability, rather than how long you had been an employee?

At the very core of unionism lies fear. Members who strongly support their union do so on the basis of fear. They are afraid of losing their jobs, losing their pay, and losing their benefits. Unions feed on the fear of their members, claiming to be their "protector" rather than encouraging individual success.

It is ironic that the same thing that attracts people to socialism, communism, and unionism, is the very thing that binds them and limits their potential as individuals: their collective fears and their belief that if they unite, they will each be protected. There is comfort in "strength in numbers" and solidarity. A united front makes individuals feel protected. However, their desire for protection is rooted in fear.

The union mentality does not reward individual effort or performance, but rather strips people of their individuality. It promotes mediocrity, although that may not be its intent. Equality ultimately trumps ability, which inevitably creates mediocrity. Union leadership assumes power from and retains power through fear. Unions offer their "protection" and tell followers they will be taken advantage of if they do not remain united. A union becomes a faceless voice for equality in which few then strive for excellence. It is fear that cripples potential, limits success, and sustains the union.

If people believed that they were truly the best at their jobs, that they were worth the highest compensation for their talents, would membership in a union make logical sense? The answer is no. A person who is the best, or strives to be the best, would prefer to shop his or her talents on an open market and sell those talents to the highest bidder. The free market is truly a person's fair share, or reflection of his or her "worth."

I do not present this argument to degrade unions or people in unions. In fact, I was once a member of a closed shop union. My wife is a current member of a teacher's union and a good number of our friends are union members as well. Many amazing and wonderful people are members of unions, and for short periods throughout history unions have served a very important role protecting workers from abuse and poor working conditions. The key words I offer are "short periods."

Over time, the societal value of unions, particularly as it relates to employee welfare, shifts from that of protection to that of exploitation; exploitation of one's employer and the exploitation of collectivist labor. Unions as an entity move from a noble and just cause to a concerted effort to amass greater power and influence. In time a union will reach a point in which it no longer serves their original and noble purpose that they were founded upon and instead take on the antisocial and counterproductive traits in which I have described. Although my position may seem on the surface as "antiunion", to assume that I am entirely against unions is untrue. I am in favor of unions as a corrective measure, to combat egregious and acute abuse of power. However, I do not believe in unionism in perpetuity as to shift the balance of power entirely from that of the employer to that of the worker(s). To do so, over a long period of time, is when unionism becomes counterproductive and damaging to society. Furthermore, I use the concept of unionism to illustrate the power of fear as it relates to employment decisions, the line of work or industries one may choose, one's livelihood, and as a result – decisions that are made in the market place.

WHAT IS FAIRNESS?

In response to feedback from many of my colleagues, it was suggested that I offer a very clear and affirming statement before outlining fairness. My statement is as followed:

> *There are some instances, and times in our lives, in which we can all use assistance. There are times in our lives in which we face economic difficulties, or personal challenges, that require support from others. However, there is and always will be a difference between necessary support to help get us back on our feet, and calculated dependence. There will always be a difference between those that are truly in need, and those that are not.*

* * * * *

In an economic sense, fairness is operating business in an environment that encourages people to choose for themselves, rather than having decisions mandated for them—or capitalism. One of the best books on capitalism was written by Adam Smith, first published in 1776, *An Inquiry into the Nature and Causes of the Wealth of Nations.*

One passage of particular interest to me and my work centers around the idea of "value." Smith contends, "The real price of everything, what every thing really costs to the man who wants to acquire it, is the toil and trouble of acquiring it. What every thing is really worth to the man who has acquired it, and who wants to dispose of it, or exchange it for something else, is the toil and trouble which it can save to himself, and which it can impose upon other people."

In short, the value of something is what a buyer is willing to pay a seller for his effort. The value of something is not what the seller thinks something is worth, or what the seller may attempt to force someone else to give for a particular item. An item may have a degree of sentimental value to someone, but that sentimental value rarely ever affects the actual monetary or exchangeable value. Furthermore, if people are forced to purchase something or are forced to pay more for it than they otherwise would willingly, this is known as coercion, not capitalism.

Capitalism can be summed up as two parties exchanging goods or services based on a mutually agreed upon value of each. Both parties walk away from the deal as willing and cooperating parties to the transaction. This sounds like "fairness" to me.

Some policy-makers are obsessed with mandates and legislating the behavior of their citizens. Other policy-makers believe that people are best equipped to make their own choices through self-determinism and a free market approach.

Let's consider commercial policy, for example. There are two principle ways in which a policy-maker can approach commerce policy-making decisions. In a free market, entrepreneurs and businesses decide for themselves how to govern their affairs. Competing businesses establish their prices based on supply and demand. Businesses may decide to market or promote their products to customers with the expectation of creating greater demand for their goods. If demand is high, generally prices will reflect demand. When businesses begin charging more than customers believe their products are worth, consumers generally stop buying. When customers stop buying, this creates a greater supply, and when supply is high and demand is low, prices necessarily fall in order to move inventory. In a free-market, capitalistic economy, businesses more or less operate under a, "you do it your way and I'll do it mine, we will see which business the customer prefers, and we will see who succeeds." Most free markets also provide some degree of legal guidelines regarding consumer protection.

At the other end of the political and economic spectrum is the so-called "nanny state," which is a socialist or communist view that seeks to legislate or mandate behavior(s). Socialism and communism attempt to determine what people can and cannot have so that all people more or less have "the same" through a cooperative management of the economy. Wages and means are not based on effort and values and exchanges are artificially manipulated through policy. Citizens are told the value of something, rather than determining that thing's value based on whether or not they are willing to pay for it.

While this may work in the short run, in the long run, both socialism and communism lead to decay in work ethic and effort. If everyone is encouraged to be equal, there is little incentive to become exceptional. "Fairness" to a socialist or communist is thus seen as what everyone has, regardless of their effort, versus what has relative to their effort. Is this really fair?

Fear is not a bad thing. We should know fear, understand our fear, and work hard to overcome our personal fear(s). We should not look to others in order to temporarily mask our fears. Relying on others for subsistence is taking the easy way out, or the path of least resistance. For many it can be, and is, tempting to rely on others. However, when it comes to "becoming" who a person truly wants to become, there is no true substitute for hard work and honest effort. Only a person's best effort, over time, will lead to success. Everything else is merely a shortcut.

As you read this, I implore you to consider your voting preferences and attempt to explain them using the METUS Principle. What are you afraid of? What causes you to affiliate yourself with one party over the other? What traits or policy preferences do you look for in a candidate for whom you vote? Why are these things important to you?

The people we vote for are a reflection of ourselves, a reflection of our values, and we should be able to clearly articulate why we vote for one person over another. If you are not able to do so, this too is telling. Do you feel lost? Do you know what you stand for? If not, does that scare you? How can you possibly live a life of peace and pursue your self-actualized self, if you know little about yourself? So again, take time to reflect. Use the METUS Principle to recognize, understand, and manage your fear. When you vote, identify what it is about a particular candidate that alleviates your fear and why that person deserves your vote. This, too, will help you learn more about yourself.

CAN FEAR MANIFEST ITSELF POSITIVELY IN A GROUP SETTING OR AMONGST THE MASSES?

The answer is yes. When individuals are able to recognize their fears, self-doubt, insecurities, and uncertainty without looking toward the group to carry them, this can be referred to as "a cause beyond one's self." Each person understands that he or she is an important piece of the group and gives his or her best effort to ensure the group's success. The success of the group has everything to do with the work of each individual. In addition, the success of the individual has nothing to do with the success of the group. In other words, each individual caused the group to achieve success, but the group did not account for the success of each individual. Each person's effort was independent of the group but contributed to the overall success.

Becoming the best of humanity means finding what it is you do best or determining what it is you want out of life. Once you are able to determine what you are good at, or what you want, you can put aside fear and work hard to achieve your own success. The worst of humanity is allowing fear to get in the way of reaching your individual potential and realizing your own success. The worst of humanity is letting fear prevent you from being your best and subsequently relying on others to provide for your basic needs. The worst of humanity is degrading, dehumanizing, and treating dependent citizens as pets rather than people.

WHY DO INCUMBENTS FARE BETTER IN ELECTIONS THAN CHALLENGERS?

The emotion of fear can explain why incumbents win reelection bids the overwhelming majority of the time. In fact, in November of 2004, 401 of the 435 sitting members of the U.S. House of Representatives sought reelection. Of those 401, all but five were reelected. In other words, incumbents seeking reelection to the House had a better than 99 percent success rate. In the U.S. Senate, only one incumbent seeking reelection was defeated. Twenty-five of twenty-six (96 percent) were reelected. (Source: http://www.cusdi.org/reelection.htm)

For decades, political scientists have pondered what factors make sitting members of Congress so hard to beat? Researchers and strategists have conducted extensive research and even written books about the "incumbent advantage" in elections. In an attempt to explain the overwhelming success of members of Congress seeking reelection, researchers have identified several factors, which make sitting members of Congress hard to beat. These factors include: the perks of the office, time, visibility, campaign organization, and money (www.thisnation.com).

While it is true each of these factors contributes to an incumbent's success, the simplest explanation, and the lowest common denominator, is fear. While an incumbent may have flaws, people take comfort in knowing what they are getting when they cast their vote. An incumbent only loses when a challenger can resoundingly convince voters that he or she is not only a great candidate, but that he or she is BETTER than the current representative. This is a major reason why dirty campaigning or mud-slinging is so successful.

Casting doubt over other candidates, their abilities, and their policy positions, can stimulate a fear response in the voter. A challenger is often a more obscure, or lesser known, figure. People may be familiar with the challenger's name, but the incumbent might have been their representative for the past two years, six years, or whatever the particular term may be. Voters like certainty, because people have a natural inclination to fear the unknown. An incumbent, even one who has flaws, is more reassuring than a challenger, which is why incumbents fare so well in reelection bids. People refer to the vote they cast as a "vote for the lesser evil," or that which they fear less.

SUMMARY

Fear shapes our societal points of view, and it influences our perceived (or real) needs. Fear becomes the lens through which we view candidates (campaigns). This explains ups and downs in polling during the course of a race. Fear, either actual or perceived, will determine how citizens will cast their votes. Fear can be, and is, manipulated in politics in order to maintain and grow voter support.

NOTES

CHAPTER EIGHT

FAITH AND FEAR

Joseph Ellwanger's Story:
Pastor, Author, and Civil Rights Leader

It is one thing to read about the civil rights movement, but quite another to speak with someone who found himself in the middle of it. Joe Ellwanger is a retired Evangelical Lutheran Church in America pastor. As the son of a pastor, Ellwanger was no stranger to residing in diverse communities. Growing up, his father served community congregations in St. Louis, MO, Waymansville, IN, and Selma, AL.

Upon graduating from Concordia Seminary in 1958, Ellwanger received his first opportunity to serve at St. Paul Lutheran in Birmingham, Alabama. It was a small African American congregation in the southwest part in the city of Titusville. Little did he know it at that time, but he would soon find himself in what he referred to in his book, *Strength for the Struggle*, as "the eye of the hurricane".

While in Birmingham, Ellwanger served as president of the Interracial Birmingham Council on Human Relations and led a group called "The Concerned White Citizens of Alabama." He also actively worked with the "Birmingham Campaign"—a movement organized by the Southern

Christian Leadership Conference (SCLC), led by Dr. Martin Luther King, Jr., to bring attention to integration efforts of African Americans.

On Saturday, March 6, 1965, Ellwanger organized a march in Selma, Alabama, to support voting rights. Along with 72 other white Alabamans, they marched on the courthouse steps in Selma, publically supporting voting rights for African Americans. It was during that time they came face to face with other white Alabamans, not to pleased with them, singing *Dixie*.

Ellwanger and his group came and left that day without any violence and he would return to march on Selma on "Turnaround Tuesday." Turnaround Tuesday was a march over the Edmund Pettus Bridge to bring attention publically to Bloody Sunday, in which 500 demonstrators were beaten back as they attempted to cross the Pettus Bridge to begin a planned march from Selma to Montgomery. Finally, following a March 12th meeting with President Lyndon Johnson, along with an interfaith group of 15 other clergy, Ellwanger along with his wife Joyce, were able to complete the final leg on their Selma to Montgomery march on March 25, 1665.

In addition to these historic events, Ellwanger also experienced violence and threats of violence in a very real and personal manner. On Sunday, September 15, 1963, the 16th Street Baptist Church in Birmingham, Alabama, was bombed. This explosion cost four young African

American girls their lives. One of these four victims, Denise McNair, was the daughter of one of Ellwanger's parishioners. In fact, Ellwanger himself was giving a service in his own church a mile down the road during the time of the bombing. He also saw many of the cross burnings presented as a show of force by the Ku Klux Klan. He personally experienced death threats – and threats to his family.

Yet, despite all of the violence going on around him; despite threats to his life and the lives of his family; despite the fact it would have been far easier for him to quietly support the civil rights movement in his heart rather than openly in public forum, Ellwanger never accepted "easy". He was committed to the movement, committed to equality for all, and proudly worked with Dr. King and other members of the African American community to raise awareness.

What may be lost in this story is that Ellwanger himself was a white man. What he was doing was not for himself, but was for others. He was willing to put his safety, and even his life, on the line as he actively engaged in the civil rights movement. For me, this offered a very interesting and compelling case, and one which I believed could be explained using the METUS Principle.

When I met Joe for the first time, in a small but well-known diner in the city of Milwaukee, I could tell that he was a special person. Because I had done my research ahead of time, I already knew what he looked like and greeted him as he walked in the door. We made our way to a booth and spent a few minutes exchanging pleasantries and getting to know each other. I explained to him that I was working on a book on motivation and found his story remarkable.

The first question I asked him was to simply hear in his own words, what it was like to live in Birmingham during the height of the civil rights movement. Without hesitation, he went on to describe what it was like for African Americans, what it was like as a white pastor with a diverse congregation, and what it was like from a civic standpoint. While listening to Joe you could get the sense that his experiences were deeply meaningful to him.

Of course, he shared the stories that most people only read about in history books, but he also reflected and talked about the emotions he felt throughout the years. It was a perspective and tone that is hard to convey in text alone. As he spoke, it was his faith and his connection to God that resonated with me. Since his faith seemed to be at the center of our conversation, I took the opportunity to ask him, "Do you believe the movement was best served through the church?" It was this single question in which Joe truly spoke to recognizing, understanding, and managing fear – and talked about the tremendous role faith played for him in the process.

Joe started to answer my question by saying, "We are all God's children and is that belief that made us all believe that equality was logical. The church not only provided a moral framework, but also gave participants courage to act. It was a sense of community, the community of God, that assured us that our efforts were just; that ours goals were just." As Joe thought about conversations of the day, he recalled the criticisms offered by others, particularly toward Dr. King, in which some believed that equality should be pursued in the courts rather than on the streets.

There were many men who felt that the public movement was creating more tension, more fighting, which was causing an even deeper divide. However, those in the church saw things differently, particularly Joe and Dr. King. However, those in the church knew that while change may be possible through the courts, promoting equality was best served through the church. By commuting a message that we are all God's children, regardless of skin color, meant that segregation now had names, faces, and souls. Equality went beyond being an intellectual or legal exercise; it was now about people...God's people... and that made the movement hard to refute or ignore.

When I asked Joe about fear, he was not shy about admitting that living in fear was a fact that he, and those engaged in the civil rights movement, experienced daily. The entire mission of the KKK was to create fear in order to manipulate and control people's behavior. If he and others capitulated, and withdrew their efforts out of fear, then the KKK would remain in control. However, if he and others were to press on, despite the threats and fear, then they took that power from the KKK.

At that moment, Joe recalled a story shared with him by Dr. King following an event in which a bomb was found in his house – and at a time in which his family's lives were threatened following the bus boycott. "It was at midnight he [Dr. King] awoke and he made himself a cup of coffee. It was at that time he received a vision, or message from God. God told him to stand up for justice and righteousness, and that He would be with him to support him." It was this vision, and message from God, that gave him the certainty to continue the movement. It was this reassurance that convinced him to remain non-violent in the face of all of the violence perpetrated around him. It was this moment that helped him answer a personal question he was struggling with, "Do you stop for safety of yourself and others [you are leading], or do you honor the crusade and your purpose?" For King the answer became abundantly clear – he had to honor his purpose.

Following Joe's story, I asked him to consider fear in an actual sense and a potential sense. I asked him, "While in the midst of the civil rights movement, what were some of your actual fears?" Joe didn't even pause to think about it, "We were afraid of bodily injury, afraid that our loved ones may be hurt, and of course, death. During those times, death wasn't just a threat; many people lost their lives, including Dr. King, eventually."

I then followed up with a second question, "What were you potentially afraid of?" This time Joe did take a moment to consider the question. Taking a sip of coffee, and tilting his head to the side, he responded, "I don't know. I suppose we felt a sense of accountability to others. We saw others that were committed to putting their own lives in harm's way, and those who lost their lives fighting for equality, and despite the risks, we didn't want to let these people down. Those of us in the church, including Dr. King, felt that we had a duty and that we were accountable to God to do something."

Those two short sentences revealed a lot about what was going through the minds of civil rights leaders during the movement. Although they actually faced personal injury, injury to their family, or even death...that fear paled in comparison to their potential fear of letting one another down—or perhaps more importantly, letting down God. Because their potential fear was greater than their actual fear, it gave them the strength and motivation to press on, to move forward, despite the risks. Their belief that their mission was just, righteous, and in line with God's wishes, solidified their sense of purpose and subsequently their actions. Even in an oppressed state, with their safety in harm's way, they found self-actualization through their purpose. In doing so, they were able to recognize, understand, and manage their fear for their mission and to achieve their purpose.

* * * * *

These things I have spoken unto you, that in me ye might have peace. In the world ye shall have tribulation: but be of good cheer; I have overcome the world.
—John 16:33

If you want to conquer your fear, don't think about yourself. Try to help others and your fear will vanish.
—Dale Carnegie

While I admit my background in religious discourse and philosophy is limited, I feel compelled to provide a brief overview of religion based on what I have learned through my readings of an assortment of scholarly works, several years of Sunday school, Gospel readings and sermons every Sunday, and conversations I have had over the years. This book would not be complete without a discussion of the many ways fear is relevant, but not exclusively limited to, religious practice. While my personal account of faith is rooted in Christianity, I do believe that it is worth noting that the concept and application of The METUS Principle is not limited to Christian faith.

RELIGIOUS EXAMPLES OF FEAR

Consider deity and how deity is presented within a particular religion. Is God described as a benevolent being or a malevolent one? Is one's God out to punish and persecute mankind or care for and love His people?

All undesirable action, or what could be described as primitive action, is rooted in fear. Such actions are our basic survival mechanism kicking in. Identify a person's underlying fear correctly and you can help that person create an action plan to address that fear. A proper diagnosis, much like any other physical or psychological condition, is critical for treating the root cause. Fear can manifest itself in many ways, and differently in different people.

Choosing to honor God, or gods, is not acting in the absence of fear, but rather is dependent on a person's ability to manage his or her fear. Since I was raised in a Catholic home, and I adhere to the principles of the Catholic faith, I will frame my discussion mostly around Christianity. However, I will attempt to interject examples from other religious faiths, or speak in a broad religious context, when possible.

When we honor God, we express reverence and appreciation for all that is [good] in our lives. Honoring God is accepting that although our lives may not be perfect, we nonetheless have things in our lives for which we choose to express thanks. I believe one's ability to appreciate what he or she has, rather than dwell on what he or she does not have, is aligned with the concept of self-actualization per Maslow.

Self-actualization does not mean you have everything you ever want, or everything you have ever wanted, but rather, self-actualization is appreciating that you have everything you need. It is the realization that one's physiological, safety, love/belonging, and esteem needs are all met. At the same time those needs are met, self-actualization inherently assumes we will stride for greater self-improvement while continuing to appreciate what we do have.

Another reason religion has played and continues to play such an influential role in people's lives is that faith and belief are things that can never be taken away from a person, as long as he or she chooses to retain it. While your neighbor can take your food, your clothes, your home, your wealth, and even your life, no one can take away your faith.

A person's faith, as far as I have been able to ascertain, is the only thing in life that can affect a person's placement on Maslow's hierarchy from the top down. People may not have food, water, shelter, or rest; they may not have safety and security; they may not feel belonging or love with their fellow man; and they may lack esteem; but

nonetheless, they may experience a self-actualized state through their faith.

From a Judeo-Christian perspective, this has been communicated to followers in John 6:35, when Jesus said, "I am the bread of life. Whoever comes to me will never go hungry, and whoever believes in me will never be thirsty." Many Christians understand this biblical verse to be a metaphor. Through the lens of the METUS Principle, I am comfortable accepting the metaphorical reference and willing to extrapolate it beyond assuming physiological needs. From a religious perspective, within the context of the METUS Principle, the verse could also read:

"I am the bread of life. Whoever comes to know me will never feel threatened...

"I am the bread of life. Whoever comes to know me will never long for love and companionship...

"I am the bread of life. Whoever comes to know me will never feel inadequate...

"I am the bread of life. Whoever comes to know me will never be less than I intend for them to be."

There are further biblical references that support this perspective that are communicated at Mass during the season of Lent. The First Reading from Exodus 17:3-7 tells a story of Moses and his struggles days after leading his people out of Egypt. The climate was dry, the sun was hot, and there was no water for them to drink. His people were afraid and close to losing hope. Moses, too, was afraid, afraid that his people would blame him for their suffering, which could very well cost him his life at their hands. When Moses asked the Lord for direction and help, his prayers were answered and he and his people were provided water.

John 4:5-42 tells a story of a woman, a Samaritan, whom Jesus quickly identified as an outcast. She traveled for water, at noon, which was near the hottest part of the day. During that time, respectable women always traveled together in groups, and went for water early in the morning before the rising sun scorched the landscape. When Jesus encountered her, he asked her for a drink. The woman was surprised that he asked her for a drink, and she quickly questioned his motive.

Jesus answered and said to her, "If you knew the gift of God and who is saying to you, 'Give me a drink, you would have asked Him and He would have given you living water."

Seeing that Jesus did not even have a bucket with him, the woman once again questioned him. Jesus answered:

> *Everyone who drinks this water will be thirsty again; but whoever drinks the water I shall give will never thirst; the water I shall give will become in him a spring of water welling up to eternal life.*

Many accounts in the Christian faith require the faithful to see beyond their physical lives and to embrace their spiritual lives, or eternal lives. For this reason, it allows believers to cast aside any actual fear in favor of potential fear. Any actual fear—absence of physiological needs, absence of safety needs, absence of love and belongingness, and absence of esteem needs—are all far less important to the faithful. It is those needs that sustain the body.

The faithful look past their actual fear to their potential fear. Their potential fear is living a life without faith, because without faith, there is no eternal life. The faithful are less concerned with the needs of the body and are focused devoutly on the needs of the soul—a soul that seeks real and everlasting life their God, His Son, and the Holy Spirit.

For this reason, the faithful are able to achieve a self-actualized state even in the most seemingly hopeless and dire conditions, because they are motivated by the needs of the soul, rather than the needs of the body. Conversely, a person who does not know God, and does not fear the absence of eternal life, will be more concerned and motivated by his or her actual fear. Such people will seek primarily or exclusively to satisfy the needs of the body, with little or no regard for the needs of the soul.

Now, I am not saying that a person can survive entirely on faith and faith alone; nor did God intend for us to do so. God gave his children, the people, resources on Earth for a reason. He intends for us to use them to sustain our bodies while remembering to feed our soul. There is no doubt a balance He expects from us, because if we could survive on faith alone, He would not have seen fit to design the complex ecology in which we find ourselves. However, what these biblical stories are designed to teach us, is that we must feed our souls and provide them with nourishment, much the same way we tend to the needs of our bodies. To reach a state of self-actualization, as Maslow described, we must see beyond our physical needs and recognize the needs of our soul.

Recognize the symptoms, ask the right questions, and you will be able to determine what a person fears. This can be seen very astutely through the prism of religion. Those who see God as a malevolent being are likely to be those who are mastered by fear. They know fear because they live in fear, and as a result, the God who created their world surely must instill fear.

Conversely, those who view their God as benevolent may acknowledge that evil exists, but also recognize their God is a God of love. A person who views God as benevolent is much more likely to have a healthy relationship with fear than one who views God as malevolent, or potentially even worse, does not acknowledge any God whatsoever.

In addition to the debate over whether or not God is a benevolent or malevolent entity, there are many other historical and cultural examples of fear overcoming rational thinking by means of human sacrifice. For example, animal and even human sacrifice in many cultures around the globe was performed as a peace offering or to appease the gods or sprits. Examples of animal and human sacrifice have been recorded in ancient Egypt, Mesopotamia, Levant, Europe, China, Tibet, India, North

America, South America, and Africa. If not for fear, the practice of sacrifice would not be necessary.

WHAT DOES "GOD-FEARING" MEAN?

Why would we fear a God who created us all, calls us His children, and holds Himself out as Father? Surely if God wanted us to fear Him, He would make it known that we are inferior to His superiority and show little interest in us other than as products of insignificant work. Yet, He aims to inspire us, teach us, guide us, and help us become better in all that we do. He does not see Himself as a ruler and people as slaves. So, again, why should any man fear God? The answer lies in understanding fear. One of the best overviews on "God-fearing" I found online at a site called *Got Questions Ministries*:

> *For the unbeliever, the fear of God is the fear of the judgment of God and eternal death, which is eternal separation from God (Luke 12:5; Hebrews 10:31). For the believer, the fear of God is something much different. The believer's fear is reverence of God. ... This reverence and awe is exactly what the fear of God means for Christians. This is the motivating factor for us to surrender to the Creator of the Universe. ... The fear of God is the basis for our walking in His ways, serving Him, and, yes, loving Him.*

From the perspective of the METUS Principle, religion requires a person to internalize something that is not visible or tangible. The natural human inclination is to fear the unknown. Yet, religion requires people to accept its premise, its rules, and its doctrine on the basis of blind faith. A faith that a higher power exists; a faith that a Higher Power created us in His image; a faith that makes certain demands, and has certain expectations, toward how we live our lives. On the surface, religion may even seem to run counter to and defy the METUS Principle. However, I assure you it does not.

King David proclaims, "The heavens declare the glory of God; the skies proclaim the work of His hands" (Psalm 19:1). It was the apostle Paul who said, "God's invisible qualities––his eternal power and divine nature––have been clearly seen, being understood from what has been made, so that men are without excuse." (Romans 1:20).

What both King David and the apostle Paul are saying is that the order and complexity of our world testifies to the existence of a higher power; of God.

Although we cannot see God Himself, a faithful believer can see Him all around us through His divine work. The true believer is able to RECOGNIZE God indirectly, through His work, and is able to embrace Him without ever actually physically seeing Him. True believers in God are able to make sense of the world around them, and UNDERSTAND such complexity in the universe simply could not be possible without a divine hand.

It is faith, and people's ability to look beyond the obvious and physically concrete nature of the world around them that allows them to MANAGE their fear through faith.

God can be seen through each of us and the work of Jesus Christ, his only Son. As Paul explains, "In Christ all the fullness of the Deity lives in bodily form" (Colossians 2:9). For Christian faithful, the incarnation of Jesus Christ is the ultimate act of God's self-revelation. Believers experience the power and presence of God in ways that are more fundamentally real than even our perceptions of the physical world. Hence, religious faith is the only human experience that can start Maslow's journey from the top down rather than the bottom up.

EASTERN VS. WESTERN RELIGIOUS PHILOSOPHY

"The War on Terror," as described from a Western perspective, is the conflict between Jihadists or other religious fanatics who will stop at nothing to destroy all that is valued in the Western world, and those who wish to preserve the Western, Christian or Judaic lifestyle. Most Americans and Western Europeans feel Jihadist sects pose a significant threat and danger to public safety and the Western way of life. In reality, they are correct in terms of practicality.

The War on Terror (also known as the Global War on Terrorism) is a term commonly applied to an international military campaign which started as a result of the 11 September 2001 terrorist attacks on the United States. This resulted in an international military campaign to eliminate al-Qaeda and other militant organizations. The

United Kingdom and many other NATO and non-NATO nations participated in the conflict.

The West has made it clear that it will oppose Middle Eastern threats through force if necessary. The West has had occupying forces in the Middle East region for decades, resulting in significant bloodshed. Each side, for different reasons, is guided by fear.

War based on religious beliefs dates back millennia. Every conflict between the opposing belief systems reaffirms their beliefs of one another. Their fear is rooted in historic, current, and projected events that cause each side to remain on high alert. These fears are very easy to recognize, and even understand, but they are exceedingly difficult to manage. However, it is not impossible.

Each side, for similar reasons, is guided by fear. From a psychological standpoint, we have a natural predisposition to fear that which a) we don't know and b) that which we do not understand. These fears are exacerbated through negative experiences. For centuries, three of the world's most popular religions—Christianity, Judaism, and Islam—have been caught up in fighting and bloodshed.

What may be a difference in faith has been compounded through war that has resulted in death and injury, annexation of land and private property, and a battle for the hearts and minds for new followers each faith needs to sustain itself. In other words, these religions are competing for a finite amount of resources. Their dislike and distrust of one another are a result of each other being a threat to physiological needs, safety needs, belonging-ness and love, esteem, and ultimately, can affect each other's ability to self-actualize.

I want to be very clear about this last point. I argue on the basis that each group can affect each other's ability to self-actualize solely on the basis that others allow them to do so. I still contend that a person can reach a self-actualized state, through religious devotion, no matter what anyone else may attempt to do to prevent him or her from doing so.

WHAT ABOUT SUICIDE?

If fear is the basis of human survival, how does fear ex-plain suicide? Many religions condemn suicide. People of Christian faith believe suicide to be a sin because only God should be able to give life and take it away. Conversely, suicide is often celebrated in the Islamic faith, particularly when a person sacrifices himself in the name of Allah.

From a perspective of mental illness, it is essential we consider perspective. What may be rational or normal to most of us may be different than to someone with a men-tal illness. A person with a mental illness may see the world completely differently than most people and their actions, perhaps irrational to the average person, are com-pletely rational to them.

French philosopher René Descartes can perhaps offer one of the best philosophical foundations for outlining perspective, and rationality. A famous quote from Des-cartes goes like this, "And so something that I thought I was seeing with my eyes is in fact grasped solely by the faculty of judgment which is in my mind." A person's rationality is just that, his and his alone. It may make little sense rationally or otherwise to someone else, but for each person is real and rational to them as is the case with those that the majority deem to be mentally ill and/or irrational. A mentally ill person may have different fears, and experience fear differently, than most people but that does not mean they do not experience fear.

The principle of fear can be used to explain suicide; even though suicide seems counter to survival and self-preservation. When individuals are driven to commit suicide, they have reached a point at which they fear something in their life more than they fear death. A person will choose death because he or she sees no other option to mitigate or relieve the fears in life. A suicidal person has been overcome with fear, and as a result, welcomes death.

HOW RELIGION MANIPULATES FEAR

When discussing religion, it is important we consider God's intent and man's intent—and that we are able to distinguish the two. I firmly believe that God, who created the Universe and could just as easily erase it from existence, has no reason to manipulate anyone. The Bible speaks of free will: Peter 3:9 says: "The Lord is not slow in keeping His promise, as some understand slowness. He is patient with you, not wanting any one to perish, but every one to come to repentance." It is God's desire for all His children to be saved. However, because He loves us, and chooses not to manipulate us, He gives us free will to choose. Either we will go to heaven, or we will not, based upon being born again or not (John 3:3).

God chose to give man free will so that He can experience true love from those whom He created, not out of obligation or fear, but out of love. When we freely chose to love God, and accept Him into our lives, that pleasure for Him is achieved. He wants man to love Him willingly. That's why God gave us free will. Not giving us free will goes against reason, for if He can do anything, forcing us to love him and honor Him would bring Him no joy. God is a logical entity; that's why He saw it right to give man the freedom to choose for himself and He hoped that we'd use our choices to give Him pleasure.

Conversely, the Devil does not have absolute power. The Devil only has power when man relinquishes to him. The Devil must use manipulation, deceit, and fear, to take the power that God bestowed upon us—free will. A prime example of the Devil manipulating man is seen in the story of Adam and Eve in the book of Genesis.

I believe it is important for people to be savvy consumers of religion and religious doctrine. It is possible for people to use religion to manipulate the behaviors of their followers. It is my position that manipulating people through religion and faith runs counter to God and more closely aligns with the Devil.

There is a difference between talking about God and inferring the word of God. I understand that reading this may seem to some as a contradiction. I assure you it is not for the following reason. When people infer the word of God, they are in essence claiming there is a right way and a wrong way to be a [Christian] and those who do not prescribe to their interpretation are violating God's wishes for His followers. Instead, I believe that faith is much more of an introspective experience; to be a very deep and personal connection between a person and his or her God.

Faith isn't for me to judge, or for you to judge, and faith is most pure when it does not infringe upon others, either physically and/or emotionally. Faith is not the absence of fear, but accepting our fear: recognizing our fear, understanding our fear. It is about turning to our faith, and to our God, and believing He will help us manage our fear to be the best version of our self. Our self-actualized self.

SUMMARY

For many, it may be very difficult to accept my premise that people can manage their fear through faith. I understand that not everyone has a deep of meaningful spiritual connection and that some dismiss religion altogether. A person's faith is a very deep, introspective connection that to some defies logic. My goal is not to convince anyone to embrace religion or that people need religion in their lives. I do not believe religion should be forced upon anyone. Instead, I believe it is up to each individual person to decide for himself or herself what role religion plays.

I do believe that religion, and more broadly faith, can play a significant role with respect to managing fear. I also believe that when looking at the METUS Principle, and attempting to explain behavior, it is important to examine the role faith plays in managing fear. As noted throughout the chapter, I believe that faith is a unique component of the human experience.

Apart from faith, we exist in a world that requires us to focus on the physical world, a world that requires each person to provide for basic needs. People must provide their body with air, water, and nutrients. Individuals must consider their safety and look out for threats. It is part of the human experience to search for love and belonging, and also to develop esteem. Each of these aforementioned aspects of the human condition is affected by a person's environmental conditions.

Faith is unique. Faith is not something that can be given to, or taken from, anyone without one's consent. A person has to decide for himself or herself whether or not to embrace and accept faith in their lives—and so long as it's desired, no one can take it away. Yet, despite our inability to quantify faith, or hold faith in our hands, it remains one of the most powerful conditions of the human experience. It is the only aspect of the human experience that can transcend basic needs and provide a person with a feeling of fulfillment; a feeling that is established when a person reaches a self-actualized state of being.

Telling a person about faith, if he or she does not know faith, is like explaining a blue sky to a blind man. A person who has never experienced sight knows nothing of color nor has a frame of reference for doing so. However, those who know faith feel it deeply. It is ingrained in every fiber of their being, whether they can articulate the feeling or not.

For these reasons, I contend that faith is a very deep, introspective, and personal experience. Faith allows people to place their fear in the hands of God or their individual Higher Power—and trust that God or the Higher Power will know what to do with it.

NOTES

FINAL THOUGHTS

The unexamined life is not worth living.
—Socrates

Develop success from failure.
Discouragement and failure are two of
the surest stepping stones to success.
—Dale Carnegie

In life, it can appear that there are many things to be fearful of. There are examples every day that reinforce many beliefs that the world we live is a scary place. However, there are countless examples that demonstrate just how amazing, and wonderful, the world is as well.

There may be times in our life we struggle to meet our basic physiological needs; there may be times in which we do not feel safe or we are not secure; there may be moments in which we long for love, or feel as if we do not belong; and there may be times in which the cruel feeling of failure grips us and brings us down. But just as time shall pass, so too will these moments – and it is up to each of us to determine what we must do in order to get us to a place in life in which we desire to be.

We all have choices. Even a person who decides to do nothing is making a choice. Life is dynamic, and the choices that we make determine the person who we are – and eventually the person who we will one day become. While some goals may be limited by some physical attributes or limitations, the reality is that by and large we possess the power to become whatever, and whomever, we aspire to be. This is very powerful and we must be mindful to never lose sight of the fact that we, and we alone, are the masters of our own destiny. Are you willing to put in the work, and make the sacrifices, that are necessary to become the person who you desire to be? Are you able to recognize, understand, and manage your fears so that you can accomplish your goals, realize your dreams, and become the person you desire to be?

As far as my little girls, Ms. Kensington Leigh and Ms. McKinley Lynnae, I will always help you in any way that I can. In doing so, each of your must also realize that you alone control your own destiny. It is my sincere hope that this book offers both of you, as well as my readers, a lens in which you may do so.

What do we live for,
if not to make life less difficult
for each other?
—George Eliot

QUOTES TO INSPIRE
FROM THOSE WHO HAVE MANAGED FEAR

Let me tell you something you already know. The world ain't all sunshine and rainbows. It is a very mean and nasty place and it will beat you to your knees and keep you there permanently if you let it. You, me, or nobody is gonna hit as hard as life. But it ain't how hard you hit; it's about how hard you can get hit, and keep moving forward. How much you can take, and keep moving forward. That's how winning is done!

Sylvester Stallone, *Rocky Balboa*

In life, the margin for error is so small. I mean one half step too late or to early you don't quite make it. One half second too slow or too fast and you don't quite catch it. The inches we need are everywhere around us. They're in every break of the game, every minute, every second.

Al Pacino, *Any Given Sunday*

Make a choice. Just decide what it's gonna be, who you're gonna be, how you are going to do it. Just decide. And from that point, the universe will get out of your way.

Will Smith, *The 5 Secrets*

You got a dream, you gotta protect it.
People can't do something themselves,
they wanna tell you that you can't do it. You want something?
Go get it. Period.

Christopher Gardner, *The Pursuit of Happyness*

Don't be afraid to fail. You can't always win,
but don't be afraid of making decisions.
Arnold Schwarzenegger, *6 Rules of Success*

He who says he can, and he who says he can't, are both usually right.
Henry Ford

Most of you say you want to be successful, but you don't want it bad.
You just kinda want it. You don't want it badder than you wanna party.
You don't want it as much as you want to be cool.
Most of you don't want success as much as you wanna sleep.
Eric Thomas, *How Bad Do You Want It Part 1, Secrets to Success Part 1*

Our deepest fear is not that we are inadequate.
Our deepest fear is that we are powerful beyond measure.
It is our light, not our darkness that most frightens us.
We ask ourselves, "Who am I to be brilliant, gorgeous, talented, fabu-
lous?" Actually, who are you not to be?
Marianne Williamson, *A Return to Love*

You have to dig deep down, dig deep down and ask yourselves, who do you
want to be? Not what, but who. Figure out for yourselves what makes you
happy, no matter how crazy it may sound to other people.
Arnold Schwarzenegger, *6 Rules of Success*

Why can't I be the best player in the league?
I don't see why [not]. Why can't I do that?
Derrick Rose

What did you say to the kid? It ain't about how hard you hit. It's about how hard you can get hit and keep moving forward. How much you can take, and keep moving forward. Get up! Get up! Get up, and don't ever give up!"
Sylvester Stallone, *Rocky Balboa*

To be able at any moment to sacrifice what we are for what we could become.
Charles Du Bos

Most of you won't be successful because when you are studying, and when you get tired, you quit.
Eric Thomas, *Secrets to Success*

Talent you have naturally.
Skill is only developed by hours and hours and hours of beating on your craft.
Will Smith

If you're not making someone else's life better, you're wasting your time.
Will Smith

Somebody came into my office crying.
I said, "Look, don't cry to give up! Cry to keep going!!"
Eric Thomas, *Secrets to Success, Part 1*

Now, if you know what you're worth, then go out and get what you're worth.
But you gotta be willing to take the hit,
and not pointing fingers saying you ain't where
you are because of him, or her, or anybody.
Cowards do that and that ain't you. You're better than that!
Sylvester Stallone, *Rocky Balboa*

Are YOU ready to recognize, understand, and manage your fear?

Are you ready to become the person you want to be?

The choice is YOURS!

REFERENCES & RESOURCES

Abram, Karen et. al (2004), "Post Traumatic Stress Disorder and Trauma in Youth Juvenile Detention." *Archives of General Psychiatry,* 61.

Aldridge and Goldman (2006). *Current Issues and Trends in Education* (2nd Edition). Pearson Education.

Aristotle., Barnes, Jonathan (1984). Complete Works of Aristotle (Volumes 1 and 2)Princeton University Press.

Caldji, Christian et al. "Maternal Care During Infancy Regulates the Development of Neural Systems Mediating the Expression of Fearfulness in the Rat" *Proceedings of the National Academy of Sciences* 95, no. 9 (April 28, 1998)

Caldji, Christian, Josie Diorio, and Michael Meaney. "Variations in Maternal Care in Infancy Regulate the Development of Stress Reactivity" *Biological Psychiatry* 48, no. 12. (December 15, 2000)

Christensen, Clayton (2012) *How Will You Measure Your Life?* New York: Harper Collins Publishing.

Collins, Jim (2001). *Good to Great.* New York: Harper Collins Publishing .

Covey, Stephen (1989). *The Seven Habits of Highly Effective People: Powerful Lessons in Personal Change.* New York: Fireside Publishing.

Cowboylyrics.com. Tim McGraw: Live Like You Were Dying. http://www.cowboylyrics.com/lyrics/mcgraw-tim/live-like-you-were-dying-13619.html

Dewey, John. 2009. "John Dewey between pragmatism and constructivism." Fordham American philosophy. Fordham University Press.

Eberhard, John. *The Tytler Cycle Revisited.* http://www.commonsensegovernment.com/article-03-14-09.html Retrieved: February 6, 2013.

Ellis, Arthur K. *Exemplars of Curriculum Theory.* (Larchment, NY: Eye on Education).

Evans, Gary and Schamberg, Michelle. (2009) "Childhood Poverty, Chronic Stress, and Adult Working Memory" *Proceedings of the National Academy of Sciences* 106, no. 16.

Felitti, Vincent. (2002) *The Relationship of Adverse Childhood Experiences to Adult Health: Turning Gold into Lead.*

Friedman, H. W., & Schustack, M. W. (2011). *Personality: Classics theories and modern research.* (5th Edition). Boston, MA: Allyn & Bacon

Fullerton, G.S. (2011). *An Introduction to Philosophy.* CreateSpace Independent Publishing Platform

Gardner, H. 1999. *Intelligence Reframed. Multiple Intelligences for the 21st Century.* New York: Basic Books.

Goethals, G.R., Worchel, S., Heatherington, L. (1999) *Pathways to Personal Growth.* Pearson Publishing.

Got Questions Ministries. What does it mean to have the fear of God? http://www.gotquestions.org/fear-God.html

Joyce, Bruce., Weil, Marsha., Calhoun, Emily. (2009) *Models of Teaching* 8th Edition. New Jersey: Pearson Education Inc.

Kail, R. V., & Cavanaugh, J. C. (2010). The Study of Human Development. Human Development: A Life-span View (5th ed.). Belmont, CA: Wadsworth Cengage Learning.

Liu, Doug et al. "Maternal Care, Hippocampal Glucocorticoid Receptors, and Hypothalamic-Pituitary-Adrenal Responses to Stress." *Science* 277, no. 5332 (September 12, 1997)

McEwen, Bruce. (2004) *Protection and Damage from Acute and Chronic Stress.* Annals from the New York Academy of Sciences 1032.

Ornstein, Allen, Hunkins, Francis. (2009) *Curriculum: Foundation, Principles, and Issues* 5th Edition. New Jersey: Pearson Education Inc.

Piaget, J., & Inhelder, B. (1973). *Memory and Intelligence.* London: Routledge and Kegan Paul.

Peters, Thomas., Waterman, Robert (2006). *In Search of Excellence.* New York: Harper Collins Publishers

Plato (1993). *The Republic*: Everyman's Library Classics & Contemporary Classics. Everyman's Library Publishing.

Santrock, John W. (2007). *A Topical Approach to Life-Span Development*. New York, NY: McGraw-Hill.

Skinner, B.F. (16 April 1984). "The operational analysis of psychological terms". *Behavioral and Brain Sciences* 7 (4): 547–81.

Slavin, Robert (2009) *Educational Psychology: Theory and Practice* (9th Edition). Pearson Education.

thisnation.com. Why are sitting members of Congress almost always reelected? http://www.thisnation.com/question/016.html. Retrieved: February 2, 2013

Tough, Paul (2012) *How Children Succeed*. Mariner Books

Weiten, Wayne (2012). *Psychology Themes and Variations* (9th Edition) Wadsworth Publishing.

Wolf, Maryanne (2007) *Proust and the Squid: The Story and the Science of the Reading Brain*. New York: Harper Collins Publishing

Wood, S.E., Wood, E.G., Boyd, D.A. (2007). *The World of Psychology* (3rd Edition) Allyn and Bacon Publishing.

Wooden, John (2005). *Wooden on Leadership*. McGraw-Hill

INDEX